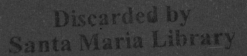

10-16-08   A.P.
mended 11-5-08   BH

99
00   01

ILL OCT 99

GAYLORD MG

PLANTING
TREES AND SHRUBS
FOR SMALL SPACES

PLANTING
TREES AND SHRUBS
FOR SMALL SPACES

A magnificent selection of dependable plants
for year-round interest in the garden

DAVID PAPWORTH • NOËL PROCKTER

CAVENDISH BOOKS
Vancouver

Preface

Trees and shrubs have a vital role to play in any garden. They provide a framework and a lasting backdrop to all the other garden plants and flowers and give a continuity throughout the four seasons of the year. Once they are established they require little or no care. They do not require constant feeding or deadheading and need only the occasional spray to offset the potential damage of pests and diseases. Even in the hottest and driest weather trees, shrubs and conifers do not require watering as their roots sink deep into the earth in search of nourishment. In fact, these plants are a godsend for the less active gardener or for those who want a low-maintenace approach. In winter both evergreen conifers and winter-flowering specimens give a wealth of interest, and in summer trees can provide a welcome haven from the heat of the sun, offering a cool vantage point to survey the splendour of a garden alive with colourful beds and borders.

Recognizing that a number of trees require a good deal of room to develop to their full potential, and also that most gardens do not provide the luxury of unlimited space, this book is designed especially for those with smaller plots, and demonstrates that, even in more confined spaces, the majesty of trees can still be enjoyed.

Around 150 specimens have been selected here and full details on planting and cultivation are included. Every plant is clearly illustrated. For anyone starting a new garden from scratch or planning a new approach to an existing design, these pages hold the key to getting the most from the great abundance of trees, shrubs and conifers which are now available.

Abelia x grandiflora
(Glossy abelia)
- **Open sunny spot**
- **Good loamy soil**
- **Late summer/early autumn flowers**

This evergreen to semi-evergreen shrub will reach a height of 1-2m/3.3-6.5ft. Its slender arching branches are slightly downy; the striking, dark green foliage has smooth, pointed leaves, 2.5-6.5cm/1-2.5in long, pale green beneath, more or less lightly toothed. The white pink-tinged funnel-shaped flowers have a faint fragrance, and are carried on the previous year's shoots in the leaf axils.

This hybrid has a good constitution and makes a vigorous graceful shrub, flowering late in the season. It does quite well on chalk and lime soils. Although there are several other abelias, *A. x grandiflora* is the most reliable. Endeavour to buy pot-grown plants.

Propagate by taking half-ripe cuttings in midsummer and insert them into a propagator with a little bottom heat.

Take care
Remove worn-out stems and very thin twigs in autumn.

Left: **Abelia** x **grandiflora**
These slightly fragrant white pink-tinged flowers are produced freely in late summer. This evergreen to semi-evergreen shrub does quite well on chalk and lime soils but needs an open sunny spot to grow to its full splendour.

Amelanchier lamarckii

(June berry, Service berry, Shad, Snowy mespilus, Sugarplum)
- **Full sun**
- **Any good soil including lime**
- **Spring flowers; autumn foliage**

This small deciduous tree or large shrub has for a long time been erroneously identified as *A. canadensis* or *A. laevis*. When grown as a small tree it needs to have a main stem about 1.2-1.5m/4-5ft before the branches start. If grown as a large shrub it can have several stems from the base. But either tree or shrub is exactly right for a small or medium-sized garden. The eventual height of a tree will be 4.5-6m/15-20ft, sometimes more.

In the spring the unfurling silky oval leaves have a coppery to pinkish hue. Before the foliage changes to a yellowish dark green, clouds of starry white flowers are scattered among the branches. Finally, in the autumn, there is a fine display of orange and red foliage. Propagate by seed, which should be sown as soon as it has been gathered, or, alternatively, by grafting in the springtime.

Take care
With standard trees, young shoots may appear up the main stem. These should be removed to retain a clean stem.

Aucuba japonica 'Variegata'

(Variegated Japanese laurel, Variegated laurel)
- **Shade or sun**
- **Any good soil, including lime**
- **Spring flowers; summer and autumn fruits**

An evergreen, 2-3m/6.5-10ft tall, with glossy yellowish spotted green foliage. The cultivar 'Variegata', which was introduced from Japan in 1783, is sometimes known as *A.j.* 'Maculata', but the true 'Maculata' is a male form, whereas 'Variegata' is female. Its small purplish flowers produce a display of oval-shaped scarlet berries, provided that there is a male form to effect pollination. Both the foliage and the berries of this plant are useful for flower arranging and make for beautiful indoor displays.

In order to have plenty of good young growth, give an annual mulch of leaf-mould, but do not fork over the ground beneath the bushes. If necessary, pruning is best carried out in early spring, and when needed a few old growths can be cut back to approximately 60cm/2ft above ground level.

This plant can be propagated by hardwood cuttings 15-23cm/6-9in long, in the autumn, inserted out of doors.

Take care
Ensure that you use sharp secateurs when pruning this plant.

Above: **Amelanchier lamarckii**
In full bloom this ornamental deciduous tree or shrub fully justifies its common name of 'Snowy mespilus' with a mass of starry white flowers borne amidst the early spring copper-tinged foliage. Grow in full sun. This tree is suitable for both small and medium-sized gardens.

Left: **Aucuba japonica 'Variegata'**
This attractive foliage shrub thrives in both sunny or shady conditions. Its small purplish flowers produce oval-shaped scarlet berries. Both the foliage and the berries are useful for floral arrangements.

11

Left: **Caryopteris** x **clandonensis** '**Heavenly Blue**'
This deciduous shrub needs some protection against harsh frosts, especially when newly planted. The dark blue flowers are produced in autumn. Prune hard each spring to encourage new growth to develop.

Caryopteris x clandonensis

(Bluebeard, Blue spiraea)
- **Sunny position**
- **Any good fertile soil**
- **Autumn flowering**

This attractive deciduous flowering shrub 1-1.5m/3.3-5ft high and 1.2-2m/4-6.5ft wide, forms a group of hybrids derived from the crossing of *C. incana* and *C. mongolica*. The cultivar 'Arthur Simmonds' has lance-shaped leaves rounded at the base, 3.5-6.5cm/1.4-2.5in long, wrinkled and dull green above, silvery-grey beneath; sometimes there are one or two outstanding teeth near the top of the leaves. Clusters of blue flowers are borne in the axils. 'Arthur Simmonds' makes a neat rounded bush about 60cm/2ft high. The cultivars 'Kew Blue' and 'Heavenly Blue' are darker in colour.

Caryopteris is hardy in most areas, but may be damaged by frost in very hard winters. Nevertheless, it needs hard pruning nearly to the base each spring. New bushes need a little protection from frost; cover them with small wigwams of canes or sacking.

Propagate by softwood cuttings during midsummer, or by half-ripe cuttings in late summer.

Take care
Protect newly planted bushes.

Purple and yellow summer flowers can just be seen amidst the foliage of this attractive specimen. The large leaves – up to 25cm/10in in length – retain their superb colour throughout the season. Grow in full sun for really bright foliage. This tree is suitable for small and medium-sized gardens.

Below: **Cercis siliquastrum**
Choose a warm sunny location and a well-drained soil for this lovely Mediterranean tree; it will not thrive in damp, cold conditions. In spring the bare branches are covered with dense clusters of pink flowers.

Catalpa bignonioides 'Aurea'

(Golden Indian bean tree)
- Sunny, sheltered situation
- Any fertile well-drained soil
- Summer and autumn foliage

The golden form of *Catalpa bignonioides*, 'Aurea', is grown for its beautiful foliage. This deciduous tree is more often grown as an outsized bush, and can each 7.6m/25ft or taller. When grown as a standard tree, 'Aurea' is grafted on to stocks of *C. bignonioides*.

The species *C. bignonioides* has foxglove-like panicles of flowers that are frilled around the edges, and speckled with purple and yellow. These flowers are followed by bean-like seedpods. The magnificent heart-shaped golden leaves of *C.b.* 'Aurea' are pointed at the tip, and are 10-25cm/4-10in long and 8-20cm/3.2-8in wide. Fortunately the yellow foliage does not become green or dull as the season advances.

Propagate the species by seeds sown under glass in the late winter, or out of doors in the spring, or by half-ripe shoots under mist spray during late summer. Prune in the winter or during early spring.

Take care
Plant young bushes or trees.

Cercis siliquastrum

(Judas tree, Love tree)
- Full sun
- Any well-drained soil
- Mid- to late spring flowering

Legend says it was on this tree that Judas hanged himself after the betrayal. Whether this is correct or not, the sight of its clusters of purplish-rose flowers is unforgettable. They are produced in spring from the joints of the old wood and on the trunks of old trees.

This deciduous tree or outsized bushy shrub reaches up to 7.6m/25ft in height, and trees nearly 100 years old will be about 9m/30ft tall. The roundish leaves are as attractive as the flowers, each having a heart-shaped base, green above and greyish below. In midsummer the flowers are followed by pea-shaped pods, 7.5-13cm/3-5in long.

This species will thrive in well-drained soils, and prefers a milder climate rather than a cold hard one. Propagate by sowing seed under glass in late winter or early spring. Remove dead wood in late winter.

Take care
Transplant at an early stage, as older plants resent disturbance.

Chimonanthus praecox

(Winter sweet)
- Sun or light shade
- Any fertile soil, except acid ones
- Flowers from midwinter

This deciduous sweetly scented shrub is often seen growing beside a wall or fence, but it can be grown as a compact free-standing shrub, reaching a height of 2.5m/8ft and equally wide. The lance-shaped leaves, 5-13cm/2-5in long, are a dark lustrous green and rough when handled. Its solitary fragrant flowers, 2-3cm/0.8-1.2in across are borne on short stalks at the joints of the previous year's shoots, from midwinter onwards. The yellowish-green flowers are purplish in the centre; the cultivar 'Luteus' is yellow without the purplish centre.

At first young bushes may not flower freely but when growth slows down, shorter flowering wood is produced, which will flower during future years. Little pruning is required for this shrub except for some thinning out.

Propagate by half-ripe cuttings of the current year's growth in summer, or by layering in spring.

Take care
Cut out surplus and weak shoots after flowering has finished.

Choisya ternata

(Mexican orange, Mexican orange blossom)
- Sheltered, sunny situation
- Not fussy over soils
- Spring flowering

This handsome evergreen shrub is suitable for all except the very coldest areas. Bushes reach a height of 2-3m/6.5-10ft. The dark green glossy leaves 8-15cm/3.2-6in long, consist of three stalkless leaflets 4-8cm/1.6-3.2in long, tapering at either end and attached to a 3-5cm/1.2-2in main stalk. When crushed, the foliage has a pungent smell, and the clusters of white spring flowers have a sweet fragrance. In winter the foliage is useful for floral arrangements.

Although it is hardy, often after frosts its foliage will look scorched, but as the weather improves so will the foliage. After frost damage, cut back shoots as necessary; if bushes have grown out of hand, cut hard back to old wood. In order to enjoy a second crop of flowers, prune back flowered shoots by about 25-30cm/10-12in as soon as blooming has finished.

Propagate by softwood cuttings taken during the summer.

Take care
Keep bushes in good shape.

Above: **Chimonanthus praecox 'Luteus'**
These delicate sweetly scented flowers brave the cold as they appear on the bare branches of this deciduous shrub from midwinter on. Grow against a sunny wall.

Below: **Choisya ternata**
This handsome shrub provides a double bonus of glossy evergreen aromatic foliage and highly fragrant spring flowers. Prune bushes after flowering to keep them in shape.

Clerodendrum trichotomum

(Glory tree)

● **Full sun**
● **Good fertile soil**
● **Late summer to early autumn flowering**

This deciduous species forms an open sparsely branched small tree or large bush 3-6m/10-20ft tall. Its large oval leaves, 10-20cm/4-8in long and 5-10cm/2-4in wide with slightly downy stalks, are arranged oppositely on the pithy branches. Fragrant white flowers are produced at the topmost pair of leaves in late summer, followed in early autumn by a reddish five-lobed calyx; in the centre of each calyx is a bright blue pea-sized berry, which eventually changes to black. The foliage has a rubbery smell when knocked or crushed, and the pithy branches and shoots continually die back.

Flowering is improved by shortening back the previous year's growth to the last pair of buds in early spring; do this every year. Propagate by suckers or root cuttings in spring.

Take care
Do not dig, fork or hoe around these bushes, as this will encourage suckers to form – unless they are wanted for propagation.

Right: **Clerodendrum trichotomum**
This display of fragrant white flowers produced in late summer is followed by an autumn show of bright blue pea-sized berries. The foliage has a distinctive aroma when knocked or crushed.

17

Cornus mas

(Cornelian cherry, Sorbet)

● Sun; will tolerate some shade
● Any good soil, including clay
● Flowers in late winter to early spring; fruit in autumn

This deciduous large shrub or small tree grows 4.5-6m/15-20ft tall. It is not a cherry, although in autumn it has bright red oblong fruits the size of a small plum, but with an acid flavour. In late winter to early spring, clusters of yellow flowers are produced, borne on the previous year's naked wood.

The branches spread almost to ground level, which makes it difficult to grow other plants beneath; however, if a leading shoot is selected from a young plant a main stem eventually develops, which will let the tree display its handsome bark. Normally little or no pruning is needed, apart from keeping the main trunk of a standard tree clean. Propagate by seeds sown out of doors in spring, but they may take two years to germinate.

Take care
Keep within bounds by careful pruning when necessary.

Left: **Cornus mas**
Bright yellow flowers cover the bare branches of this shrub or small tree as winter turns to spring. In autumn it has bright red fruits. Another attractive feature is its handsome bark.

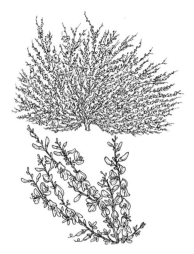

Below: **Cotoneaster horizontalis**
Profuse red berries light up this hardy and adaptable shrub during the autumn as the glossy green leaves turn to orange and red. Excellent on walls, banks and as ground cover.

Cotoneaster horizontalis

(Fishbone cotoneaster, Herringbone cotoneaster, Rock cotoneaster)
● **Sun or partial shade**
● **Any good soil, including chalk**
● **Spring flowers; autumn colour**

This low-growing deciduous cotoneaster gets its common names because the bare horizontal branches look rather like the bones of a fish. It has dark glossy green leaves above, mostly smooth beneath though sometimes with a few scattered hairs; the leaves are 6-12mm/0.25-0.5in long, and 2cm/0.8in wide.

In the spring the white flowers suffused with pink are a great attraction to bees seeking nectar. In the autumn there are bright red berries, and the dark green foliage changes to various shades of orange and red before it finally falls. This is an excellent low-growing shrub for ground cover or to clothe banks. Bushes will reach a height of 60-90cm/2-3ft. The cultivar 'Variegatus' has leaves which are attractively edged with white.

Propagate by seed which should be stratified (stored damp to soften the seed coat) and sown in spring, or by half-ripe cuttings in summer or hardwood cuttings in autumn.

Take care
Cut out dead shoots in late winter.

Cytisus scoparius

(Broom, Common broom, Scotch broom)
● **Full sun**
● **Any good deep soil, but avoid chalky soils**
● **Spring flowering**

The common broom is a free-flowering deciduous shrub, but when the foliage has fallen the green stems give an evergreen appearance. The shrub reaches a height of 1.5-2m/5-6.5ft and as much in width.

The hybrids prefer a deep soil, neutral or slightly acid, but not poor shallow soils. They like plenty of sun. The variety 'Golden Sunlight' grows 60cm/2ft high and 90cm/3ft wide; above the dark, dull green foliage, orange-yellow flowers (singly or in pairs) appear on 30-45cm/12-18in inflorescences in spring. The many varieties also include the yellow and crimson flowered 'Andreanus'; the cream and yellow 'Cornish Cream'; and the lovely 1.5m/5ft 'Burkwoodii' in varying shades of maroon, purple and red. The range of colours is wide.

The only pruning required is to cut off roughly two-thirds of the previous year's shoots.

Propagate by seed sown out of doors in spring, or by heel or nodal cuttings during summer.

Take care
Do not cut into old wood.

Right: **Cytisus scoparius**
The rich yellow flowers of this strong growing variety glow in the spring sunshine. There are many varieties in a range of colours from maroon to purple and red.

Right: **Daphne** x **burkwoodii 'Somerset'**
In a moist but well-drained soil this semi-evergreen shrub is covered with fragrant blush-pink blooms during spring and early summer. It thrives in a sandy loam.

Daphne x burkwoodii 'Somerset'

● **Full sunshine**
● **A well-drained moist soil**
● **Flowers late spring to early summer**

The semi-evergreen or almost deciduous shrub 'Somerset' is a clone of *D. x burkwoodii*. It reaches about 1m/39in in height and makes a sparingly branched bush with 2.5cm/1in almost lance-shaped leaves. This clone has sweetly scented blush-pink tubular flowers, the outside flushed with rose, and produced in bunches of six on short lateral shoots.

Like most daphnes 'Somerset' likes good drainage, yet it must have an ample supply of moisture. Dryness at the roots must be avoided if the shrub is to thrive in the garden. 'Somerset' does well on a sandy loam.

As daphnes transplant badly, always obtain young container grown plants, which should be planted in their permanent positions as soon as possible. Propagate by half-ripe cuttings during the summer.

Take care
Prevent dryness at the roots.

Daphne mezereum

(February daphne, Mezereon)
- **Sun, but tolerates some shade**
- **Any good fertile soil**
- **Flowers late winter or early spring**

When *Daphne mezereum* blooms in late winter, it tells us that spring is just around the corner. This colourful and fragrant deciduous shrub reaches a height of 1-1.5m/3.3-5ft and as much in width. Spear-like leaves taper at the base and are either pointed or rounded at the apex; they are 4-9cm/1.6-3.5in long and 6-20mm/-0.25-0.8in wide. The sweetly scented purplish-red flowers are produced in twos and threes on erect naked wood. The green berries later become bright red, and these are attractive to blackbirds.

As this is not a long-lived shrub, have a few seedlings or plants from cuttings available in case of losses. Usually a few berries drop, and some will germinate. Propagate by seed when it is ripe, or by taking nearly ripe cuttings in the early autumn Usually no pruning is needed, but if a shoot needs cutting in order to improve the shape of the bush, do this in the spring.

Take care
Be sure to have young plants available as replacements.

Daphne odora 'Aureomarginata'

(Winter daphne)
- **Full sun**
- **Any well-drained soil**
- **Flowers late winter or early spring**

This evergreen shrub has a delicious fragrance. The cultivar 'Aureomarginata' is hardier and more vigorous than the species. Even so, in cold areas choose a sheltered position; otherwise any good open site will suffice. It can be grown successfully in a well-drained clay soil and also where there is chalk in the soil, although it does not really need it.

The narrow oval leaves, 4-9cm/1.6-3.5in long, are faintly margined in creamy-white. The flowers, reddish-purple on the outside and paler within, are sweetly scented; one plant will scent the entire garden in late winter and early spring. This shrub will grow to 1.2-1.8m/4-6ft tall, and about the same in width.

Propagate by layering or by taking half-ripe cuttings of the current year's growth during midsummer.

Take care
Prune after flowering, but only when really necessary.

Above left: **Daphne mezereum**
These scented flower clusters are produced in very early spring on the bare branches. They are replaced in summer and autumn by green berries that gradually turn bright red.

Above: **Daphne odora 'Aureomarginata'**
Highly fragrant flowers are borne amidst foliage which is faintly margined in a creamy-white border. One plant will scent the whole garden during late winter and early springtime.

Deutzia x elegantissima 'Fasciculata'
- Sunny situation
- Good loamy soil; tolerates lime
- Spring flowering

Deutzias are deciduous shrubs, with panicles of dainty flowers in spring. They need ample moisture and good loamy soil; the majority tolerate lime. 'Fasciculata' makes a graceful shrub up to 1.5m/5ft tall. Deutzias are wiry shrubs, and their oval-shaped foliage is rather wrinkled. The flowers are borne on the previous year's growth; they are almost 2.5cm/1in wide, bright rosy-pink on the outside and pale within. Another equally beautiful deutzia is 'Rosealind', which has deep carmine flowers.

Every two years, thin out old flowering shoots and any dead branches. Although deutzias are winter-hardy, they make rather early growth, and in frost pockets or low-lying districts they can become frosted.

Propagate by half-ripe cuttings inserted where there is gentle bottom heat during early to mid-summer, or by hardwood cuttings inserted out of doors in autumn.

Take care
Provide ample moisture.

Embothrium coccineum
(Chilean firebush, Chilean fire tree)
- Shade
- Moist loamy lime-free soil
- Flowers in spring and early summer

This showy evergreen shrub or small tree is sometimes, though rarely, semi-deciduous. It must have a cool root run, which can be achieved where there is a moist loamy soil, free of lime or chalk. Also it must be furnished with shelter from cold drying winds. Provided it has shelter, and a modicum of shade from surrounding trees, it should eventually give a spectacular display of brilliant orange-scarlet flowers during the spring and into the early summer months. The dark glossy green leaves are greyish-green above and paler beneath. As a bush it will reach to a height of up to 3.6-4.5m/12-15ft, and as a tree it grows to 7.6-9m/25-30ft high. No pruning is necessary for this plant.

Propagate by seeds sown in late winter under glass, or by root cuttings taken in winter and inserted in small pots where there is moderate bottom heat.

Take care
Choose a sheltered situation, as these trees are

Enkianthus campanulatus
- Full sun
- Moist loamy lime-free soil
- Spring flowers; autumn foliage

When young this hardy deciduous shrub has a slightly erect habit, but as it develops it becomes a densely branched bushy shrub, which normally requires no pruning. It can reach a height of 1.5-2.7m/5-9ft and almost as much in width. The finely-toothed dull-green leaves are 2.5-6.5cm/ 1-2.5in long and 1.2-3.5cm/0.5-1.4in wide. The bell-shaped creamy-yellow pendulous flowers, veined and red-tipped, form pretty clusters, each flower on an 8mm/0.3in stalk. The flowers are produced in spring on the terminal buds of the previous year's shoots. In autumn, the foliage changes to attractive shades of yellow and red.

Enkianthus needs a cool moist peaty soil. When bushes become overgrown or misshapen, cut them hard back. Provided new growth appears from the base, all is well.

Propagate by seed under glass in the late winter, by softwood cuttings in the summer, or by layering in the spring.

Take care
Note whether plenty of new growth is appearing from the base.

Far left: **Deutzia** x **elegantissima 'Fasciculata'**
An easy-care deciduous shrub grown for its dainty spring flowers which are rosy-pink on the outside and pale inside. Needs good sunshine.

Left: **Embothrium coccineum**
These fiery flowers are produced during spring and early summer. This evergreen bush needs shelter from cold winds, and a lime-free soil.

Below: **Enkianthus campanulatus**
These bell-shaped flowers adorn the shrub in the spring. The autumn foliage changes to attractive shades of yellow and red.

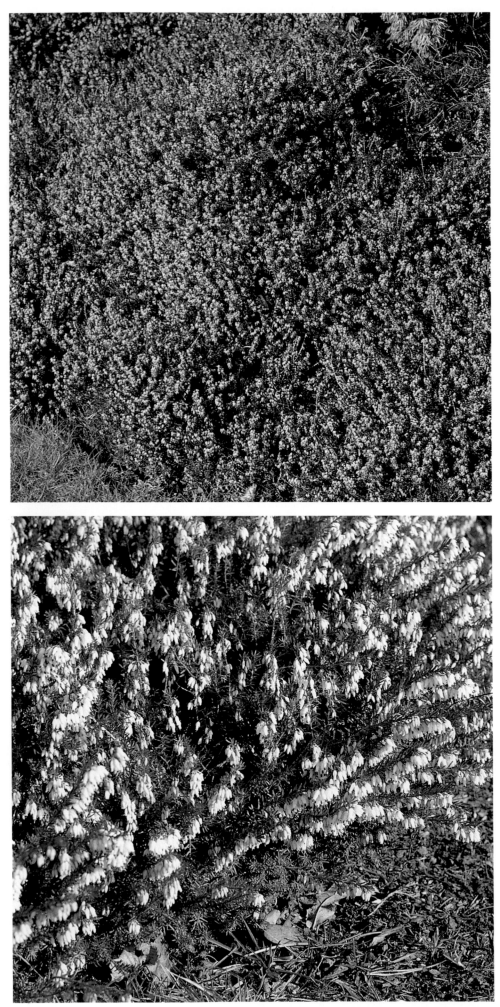

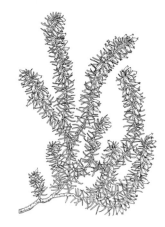

Erica carnea
(E. herbacea)
(Winter heather, Snow heather)
- **Open sunny situation**
- **Light soil; tolerates lime**
- **Autumn to spring flowers**

This attractive species offers a wide variety of colours, from white, pink, red, and rosy-purple to dark carmine red. The cultivar 'December Red', 15-23cm/6-9in high, has bright rose-pink flowers above a mat of dark green leaves from early winter. 'Springwood White' is the same height with light green foliage and long white spikes.

Choose an open situation and avoid rich soils. Plant deeply, i.e. with the lowest foliage resting on the soil, in early spring. The tufted shrubs produce tight hummocks 15-30cm/6-12in high, forming prostrate spreading plants. The small dark glossy green foliage is usually arranged in whorls of four. Flowers are produced singly or in pairs, in the leaf axils of the previous year's growth. With shears trim all faded blooms after flowering has finished.

Propagate by heel or nodal cuttings in late summer, or by layering in spring.

Take care
Moisten peat before use.

Above left: **Erica carnea 'December Red'**
An attractive winter-flowering heather suitable for open spots and for light soils. It produces rose-pink flowers above dark green leaves from late autumn/early winter.

Left: **Erica carnea 'Springwood White'**
This cultivar has light green foliage and long white spikes. The species as a whole offers an extensive range of colours and provides interest throughout the winter months.

Below: **Escallonia 'C.F. Ball'**
A free-flowering plant, it produces large red flowers from summer to early autumn, making a fine display. It will reach up to 2.5m/8ft in height and is excellent for seaside areas.

Escallonia

- Sun loving
- Well-drained soil; tolerates lime
- Summer flowering

The evergreen escallonias are not considered completely hardy. In particularly cold areas they go to 'sleep' earlier and 'wake up' later than those in warmer regions, where they flower up to midwinter and then are frosted in the late wintertime.

The following two hybrids are especially recommended as suitable for the majority of gardens. 'Apple Blossom' is a slow-growing variety with pink and white flowers; it reaches a height of 1.5-2m/5-6ft. 'C.F. Ball' is a free-flowering and strong-growing escallonia, which produces large red flowers from the summer to the early autumn; it will reach a height 2.1-2.5m/7-8ft in favoured localities.

Both these escallonias do well by the sea, as they all do. No regular pruning is required; cut back occasionally after flowering to keep bushes shapely, or do it in spring. Escallonias flower on one-year-old wood.

Propagate this plant by half-ripe cuttings during the summer, or by seed which is sown in the late winter under glass.

Take care
The soil must not be too rich.

Forsythia x intermedia 'Spectabilis'

(Golden Bells)
- Full sun
- Any good soil, even chalk
- Spring flowering

This hardy deciduous shrub, 2.5-3m/8-10ft tall and almost as wide, is known to most gardeners for its colourful display in spring. The bright yellow flowers are borne singly or in twos and threes in the axils of the broad lance-shaped leaves. 'Spectabilis' has large rich yellow flowers. 'Lynwood' has even larger broad-petalled flowers.

Forsythias do not seem to mind how much they are pruned, but if cut hard back every year they will not produce many flowers. New shoots, made after the flowers have faded, will bud up during the year and flower the following spring. Each year cut out a few of the oldest growths to encourage new wood from the base; if this is not done, a mass of twiggy growth accumulates in the centre of a bush, which causes non- or poor flowering wood. Cut newly planted bushes back to within 30cm/1ft of ground level.

Propagate by softwood cuttings in the summer with heat, or, alternatively, take hardwood cuttings in the autumn.

Take care
Cut old growth after flowering.

Right: **Forsythia x intermedia 'Spectabilis'**
In spring the emerging leaves of this deciduous shrub are joined by bright yellow flowers that provide welcome colour in the garden. Prune carefully to encourage blooms.

Left: **Garrya elliptica**

In the protection of a sunny wall, where it can receive good light, the male plant of this evergreen shrub will put on a striking show of long catkins in late winter.

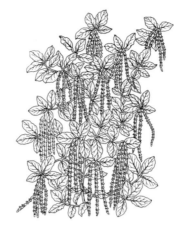

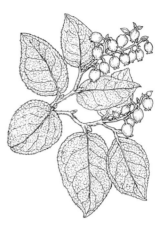

Garrya elliptica

(Silk tassel bush)
- **Sunny location**
- **Ordinary soil, but moisture-holding**
- **Catkins early to late winter**

A striking evergreen catkin-bearing shrub that thrives in the protection of a wall where it can receive good light. In favoured areas, bushes reach as much as 5m/16.4ft tall. The oval wavy-margined leathery leaves, 4-8cm/1.6-3.2in long, are matt grey-green above and woolly underneath. In the winter the bush has attractive pendent greyish-green male catkins which are 15-25cm/6-10in long; when these are brushed or shaken a shower of soft yellowish-green pollen is produced.

This shrub does not require a rich soil, but should have plenty of sun and moisture. Choose pot-grown plants, as it is not a good transplanter, so small plants are preferable to large ones. Little or no pruning is needed.

Propagate by seeds sown in the spring in a cool greenhouse. For male plants, grafting is necessary during the late winter under glass in heat. Layering is possible in the summer.

Take care

Do not be too generous with manure. It is also important not to allow the plants to become dry at the roots.

Gaultheria shallon

(Salal, Shallon)
- **Sun or shade**
- **Lime-free, peaty and acid soils**
- **Flowers in late spring to early summer, fruits in autumn**

This useful hardy evergreen shrub forms a dense thicket, sending up many stems from the base; it reaches a height of 71cm-2m/28in-6.5ft. It spreads by underground stems. The young reddish bristly branches later become rough with age. The leathery dark green leaves are attached to reddish hairy stalks. The pinkish-white egg-shaped flowers are produced in late spring to early summer, and followed in late summer and autumn by dark purple berries.

This is an ideal shrub where a dense evergreen thicket or ground cover is needed in moist, shady areas. As a rule little pruning is needed except cutting out dead stems or reducing live ones with secateurs. If the plant becomes too dense, chunks can be cut out with a sharp spade.

Propagate by division in spring, by seeds sown under glass in late winter or out of doors in early spring, or by layering in the autumn.

Take care

Do not let this species overrun any precious shrubs nearby.

Below: **Gaultheria shallon**

An excellent evergreen shrub where a dense thicket or gound cover is required in moist, lime-free soil. The pinkish-white flowers are produced in late spring to early summer, followed in autumn by purple berries.

Genista lydia

- Full sun
- Well-drained soil; tolerates lime
- Flowers in late spring to early summer

This hummock-forming deciduous shrub will reach a height of 80cm/32in. The bright golden-yellow flowers are produced usually in clusters of four at the end of leafy twigs on pendulous green five-angled branches during the period of late spring and early summer.

It will tolerate lime, but this is by no means essential. What it does need is a well-drained, sunny position. Although hardy, plants may succumb after a mild wet autumn followed by early winter frosts or late spring frosts; when this happens, scrap the plant and start afresh. Where more compact plants are needed, light pruning can be given as soon as the flowers fade.

Propagate by seeds sown under glass in late winter or out of doors in early spring. Heel cuttings can be taken during the summer.

Take care
Choose a well-drained position which is protected from draughts.

Helianthemum 'Rhodanthe Carneum'

(Sun rose, Rock rose)
- Full sun
- Any good garden soil
- Flowering late spring to just after midsummer

The hybrid 'Rhodanthe Carneum' has soft wild-rose-pink flowers with an orange-yellow centre, and silver-grey foliage. It makes a fine clump 23-30cm/9-12in high, and will spread to as much as 80cm/32in across. 'Henfield Brilliant' has glistening brick-red flowers that cover a hummock of silver-green foliage, silvery beneath; its dimensions are the same as those of 'Rhodanthe Carneum'. 'Wisley Pink' has pale pink flowers with an orange-yellow centre, and grey foliage.

The only pruning needed is to cut off old flowerheads and shorten long straggly shoots; from time to time it may be necessary to give the whole plant a trim over with a pair of secateurs.

Propagate during mid- to late summer by half-ripe cuttings, with or without a heel, inserted in a cold frame.

Take care
Keep plants healthy by careful trimming when needed.

Kalmia latifolia

(Calico bush, Ivy bush, Mountain laurel, Spoonwood)
- Full sun or light shade
- Moist fertile peaty soil; not chalk or lime
- Early summer flowering

Surely one of the most beautiful evergreen shrubs, with an affinity to a rhododendron, and a lover of acid peaty soil. A single specimen can reach a height of 3m/10ft with a similar width. Its large oval leathery leaves are a rich glossy green. A well-grown bush forms dense thickets. The pink ten-ribbed flowers, each one like the inside of a parasol, are borne in superbly delicate clusters in early summer.

To flourish, this shrub needs moist well-drained peaty soil, above all lime-free – in full sun or light shade. When it fails, the fault is usually unsuitable growing conditions. No regular pruning is needed. Should a bush grow out of hand it can be pruned hard back in spring, but it takes some time to regenerate new growth.

Propagate by seed sown in spring under glass, but this is not an easy plant to propagate. Half-ripe cuttings taken in late summer can sometimes be successful.

Take care
Give sufficient moisture.

Left: **Genista lydia**
This crop of bright yellow flowers appears in early summer. The plant spreads freely in hummocks about 80cm/32in high and enjoys a sunny situation on well-drained, fairly poor soils. It needs to be protected against frost.

Above: **Helianthemum 'Rhodanthe Carneum'**
The silver-grey foliage acts as the perfect foil for these rose-pink flowers with their orange-yellow centres. It makes a fine clump and is an ideal plant for dry sunny banks.

Right: **Kalmia latifolia**
Beautiful in bloom and handsome in leaf, this evergreen shrub thrives in moist lime-free soils. The pink flowers, each resembling the inside of a parasol, form clusters in early summer.

Kerria japonica 'Pleniflora'

(Japanese rose, Jew's mallow)
● **Full sun**
● **Any good garden soil, including chalk**
● **Spring flowering**

A useful deciduous hardy shrub, which has apple-green bamboo-like branches and shoots that bear bright orange-yellow double pompom flowers, 4cm/1.6in across or sometimes more. It will reach a height of 2.5-3m/8-10ft. It spreads very freely by underground stoloniferous roots, which in turn send up new shoots. This vigorous shrub not only has attractive flowers and apple-green branches, but in autumn its leaves turn an attractive light yellow.

Prune after flowering by cutting flowering wood, and reduce unwanted shoots. Propagate by hardwood cuttings in autumn, or by division of sucker growths in spring.

Take care
Remove all unwanted sucker shoots that appear, before they encroach on other shrubs or perennials.

Right: **Kolkwitzia amabilis 'Pink Cloud'**
The variety name aptly describes this early summer floral display of dense clusters of bell-shaped flowers. This hardy shrub is particularly useful if the garden has a chalky soil.

Below: **Koelreuteria paniculata**
These handsome pinnate leaves can be 45cm/18in long. In late summer, this medium-sized tree bears impressive clusters of bright yellow blooms. Grow it in full sun.

Koelreuteria paniculata

(China tree, Golden rain tree, Pride of India, Varnish tree)
● **Full sun**
● **Any good loamy soil**
● **Late summer flowers; autumn foliage**

This handsome slow-growing deciduous ornamental tree can reach 3-4.5m/10-15ft high, or even up to 9m/30ft. It is a tree that should be grown much more than it is. Its alternate pinnate leaves have nine to 15 leaflets, or sometimes they are bipinnate. The total length of each leaf can be as much as 45cm/18in. The yellow flowers are borne in large terminal pyramidal panicles up to 30cm/1ft long, and produced in late summer. These are followed by bladder-like fruits. In autumn the foliage turns a bright yellow.

Standard trees can be purchased from reputable nurserymen, with a stem 1.2-1.5m/4-5ft tall before the head of branches commences. This tree must be grown in full sunshine. No pruning is required, apart from keeping the main stem clean.

Propagate by seeds sown in spring, or by root cuttings taken in winter and grown under glass.

Take care
Give this tree full sun.

Kolkwitzia amabilis 'Pink Cloud'

(Beauty bush)
● **Sunny position**
● **Any good soil, including chalk**
● **Flowers in spring and early summer**

This handsome deciduous hardy shrub, 2-2.5m/6.5-8ft high, forms a dense twiggy bush, most suitable for a medium-sized garden. The opposite leaves are roughly oval, and rounded at the base, dull green above and paler beneath. In the spring and during the early summer the arching branches are covered with dense clusters of bell-shaped flowers; the roundish lobes are pink, the throat a delicate yellow. One of the best clones which has been produced for garden use is 'Pink Cloud', which has the same colouring as the species.

The only pruning needed is to remove old or weak wood as soon as the bushes have finished flowering, but always bear in mind that kolkwitzias should be allowed to grow naturally.

Propagate by taking half-ripe cuttings in summer; insert them in a propagating frame with some bottom heat.

Take care
Do not over-prune.

31

Laburnum anagyroides
(Common laburnum)

- Sunny location
- Any garden soil
- Flowers in late spring and early summer

Laburnum is one of the most popular small deciduous flowering trees for a late spring and early summer display of colour. It will reach a height of 5.5-7.6m/18-25ft. The trifoliate leaves have a long stalk and oval leaflets, dull green above and downy beneath. The golden-yellow flowers are borne on downy pendulous racemes, 15-25cm/6-10in long.

As laburnums bloom so freely they also set seed freely, and this can be a strain on the tree. Therefore as soon as flowering has finished remove the seedpods. Laburnums are not especially long-lived trees. Where there are young children it is a wise precaution to remove the seedpods, because they are poisonous. This is a tree that needs secure staking, especially when young or newly planted. If large branches have to be removed, do this in summer; if it is done in spring, bleeding can occur.

Propagate by seeds in spring.

Take care
Stake trees securely.

Right: **Laburnum anagyroides**
Trained over a garden pergola, these pendulous racemes of late spring flowers form a striking floral canopy. A handsome tree but beware – all parts of it are poisonous.

Below: **Lavendula 'Hidcote'**
The heady fragrance of the lavender's flowers and foliage is reason enough to recommend it for garden use. It is also excellent as an edging plant on light soils in open locations.

Laburnum x watereri

(Golden rain)
● Sunny location
● Any garden soil
● Early summer flowering

This hardy deciduous flowering tree is a hybrid between *L. alpinum* and *L. anagyroides*, and it makes a small compact tree with glossy green trifoliate leaves. It produces slender 30cm/1ft racemes of yellow fragrant flowers in the early summer months.

The seeds of laburnum species are poisonous so care should be taken, but *L. x watereri* has the advantage that seed does not set so freely on this hybrid as it does on the common laburnum. Another equally beautiful cross which has the same parent as *L. x watereri* is the cultivar 'Vossii', which has even longer racemes of golden-yellow flowers, reaching up to 71cm/28in in length. Trees will eventually reach a height of approximately 9-10.7m/30-35ft.

Like all laburnums, in the early stages of their life they must be given secure staking. Prune as for *L. anagyroides*.

Propagate by grafting on to *L. anagyroides* during the spring.

Take care
Stake trees securely.

Lavandula 'Hidcote'

(Lavender)
● Full sun
● Light, not too rich soil, including chalky soils
● Early summer flowering

The evergreen low-growing fragrant-foliaged early-flowering lavenders, such as 'Hidcote' and 'Munstead', are very useful for a small garden, either as a clump of three or four plants or as a low edging or hedge by a flower border, especially around rosebeds. 'Hidcote' will reach a height of 25-38cm/10-15in, forming a compact small bush. It has narrow grey-green foliage, and stems which in early summer produce close spikes of violet-coloured flowers.

Lavenders thrive best on a light, not-too-rich soil and grow well in chalk or lime soils. The best time to prune lavender is in the spring, but do not prune immediately after flowering, because the old growth protects the young growth, which will produce the next year's crop of flowers.

Propagate by taking heel or nodal cuttings of ripened wood; insert them in sandy soil in a cold frame in late summer.

Take care
Do not prune after flowering, but wait until the following spring.

Left: **Laburnum x watereri**
In an open sunny location, this compact garden tree puts on a marvellous show of pendulous yellow flowers in early summer. As a bonus, the flowers are fragrant and rarely set seed. Stake young trees securely.

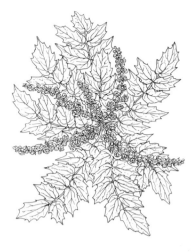

Lonicera x purpusii

- Full sun
- Any good garden soil
- Winter flowering

This very attractive deciduous hardy flowering shrub is a hybrid between *L. fragantissima* and *L. standishii*. The creamy-white fragrant flowers, in clusters of two to four, are carried in the axils of the opposite foliage. The leaves are oval in shape, 5-9cm/2-3.5in long and 3-4.5cm/1.2-1.8in wide, somewhat rounded at the base and edged with bristly hairs. The joy about this shrub is that it produces flowers and a distinctive fragrance during the late winter. It is also taller than either of its parents and will eventually reach a height of up to 3m/10ft and larger in width.

The only pruning needed is to thin and shorten any extra-long branches after the flowering period is over.

Propagate by taking cuttings of mature wood of the current season's growth, with or without a heel, and about 20-30cm/8-12in long; insert out of doors in an open border.

Take care
It is necessary to keep this vigorous shrub within acceptable bounds, otherwise it may invade other parts of the garden.

Magnolia stellata

(Star magnolia)
- Sunny position
- Good loam or peaty soil
- Spring flowering

This is the ideal deciduous shrub for a small garden where a magnolia is desired. It makes a compact rounded shrub, 2.5-3.6m/8-12ft tall and as much or sometimes more in width. The long narrow oblong leaves are 6.5-10cm/2.5-4in in length. In spring the bush produces fragrant, pure white strap-like flowers, each flower having 12 to 18 petals.

This plant needs a sunny position and a good loamy soil, with added leaf-mould, peat and sand if the ground is at all wet or inclined to drain badly. Initial preparation prior to planting is essential. Newly planted bushes will take up to two years to establish. This species is easily blackened by the frost, so try to plant it in a sheltered position within the garden. No pruning is necessary.

Propagate this superb shrub by layering·in early spring.

Take care
Choose a sheltered situation to avoid frost damage.

Mahonia japonica

- Sun or dappled shade
- Good loam or peaty soil
- Winter flowering

This evergreen shrub is probably one of the most popular because it flowers in winter. The lemon-yellow fragrant flowers, 20-25cm/8-10in long, are borne on pendulous racemes in clusters of ten or more at the tips of the previous year's growth. The leaves, dark green above and yellowish beneath, are 30-45cm/12-18in long with 13 to 19 leaflets, each spine-tipped at the apex. When first planted, bushes seem slow to start; but once established they soon put on growth and eventually reach a height of 1.5-2.1m/5-7ft. This is a stiff-growing shrub and sparsely branched, but when well grown it becomes a superb asset to any shrub border.

No regular pruning is needed, but a few sprays cut for indoor displays will encourage new growth in the main shrub.

Propagate by taking half-ripe cuttings of the current year's growth during summer, making them about 15cm/6in long.

Take care
Give this mahonia enough room to spread naturally.

Left: **Lonicera x purpusii**
Creamy-white fragrant flowers are carried on almost bare branches in late winter. This shrub grows vigorously and must be kept in check by pruning after flowering is over.

Left: Magnolia stellata
This compact slow-growing deciduous shrub bears a splendid display of creamy-white fragrant flowers in spring. Grow it in a good soil fortified with leaf-mould and peat.

Below: Mahonia japonica
This evergreen shrub will grow happily in light shade. Its pale lemon-yellow scented flowers appear in winter, making it very popular with gardeners. It requires a good loam or peaty soil.

Osmanthus x burkwoodii
(Osmarea x burkwoodii)
- **Sun or light shade**
- **Any good loamy or chalk soil**
- **Spring flowering**

This hardy evergreen shrub was originally known as a bigeneric hybrid between *Osmanthus delavayi* and *Phillyrea decora*, but since the second parent is now called *Osmanthus decorus*, botanists have decreed that the shrub is a hybrid between *O. delavayi* and *O. decorus*. Whichever name it is sold under, buy it, for it is a real beauty. It has glossy oval dark olive-green toothed leaves, 2.5-5cm/1-2in long. The terminal and axillary clusters of six or seven fragrant white flowers are produced in the spring; they are not so sweetly scented as *O. delavayi*, but hardier. It is rather slow in growth, but eventually makes a dense bushy shrub, 2.7-3.6m/9-12ft in height and equally wide. It is a desirable and useful plant for any garden.

Any pruning needed should be done once flowering has finished. Propagate by half-ripe cuttings, in late spring or early summer.

Take care
Give plenty of room to expand.

Osmanthus delavayi
- **Sun or light shade**
- **Any good loamy or chalk soil**
- **Spring flowering**

This evergreen shrub has sweetly scented flowers. It is hardy except in the very coldest and frostiest areas, where it should be grown against a wall or fence. It has small dark green leathery leaves, with tiny dark spots beneath; the leaves are oval in shape and tapered at each end. In spring it has pure white fragrant jasmine-like flowers, which are produced in terminal and axillary clusters. In favoured localities it will reach a height of 3m/10ft, and sometimes more in overall width.

Plant this shrub where it will have protection from the overhanging branches of a nearby tree, or in a position where the sun will not reach the bush before the frost is off, so that damage to the flowers will be less. Any pruning should be done after flowering.

Propagate by half-ripe cuttings taken in the late summer.

Take care
Plant this shrub in a position which affords some protection.

Paeonia suffruticosa
(Peony, Tree peony)
- **Some shade is preferable**
- **Any good garden soil**
- **Spring flowering**

This hardy deciduous flowering shrub is a slow grower, eventually reaching a height of 1.2-1.5m/4-5ft, sometimes 2m/6.5ft and equally wide. It has gnarled twisted branches with elegant foliage; the doubly pinnate or double ternate leaves are 23-45cm/9-18in long, dark to mid-green above and bluish-grey beneath. The 15cm/6in wide flowers are white with a maroon-purple blotch at the base of each petal. *P.s.* 'Rock's Variety' is similar in colour.

Tree peonies need a protected position so that the early morning sun does not harm the blooms before any frost on them has thawed. Peonies need rich well-cultivated soil with liberal mulchings of leaf-mould or well-rotted farmyard manure. The only pruning necessary is to remove any dead wood after flowering. Propagate by grafting on to rootstocks of *P. officinalis* in spring.

Take care
Shade peonies to prevent frost damage.

Far left: **Osmanthus** x **burkwoodii**
This hybrid has dark glossy leaves and is hardy. It grows slowy into a dense bush, thrives in any soil, including chalk, and can stand light shade.

Left: **Osmanthus delavayi**
These white flowers, superbly fragrant, appear in early spring. The shrub grows in almost any soil and situation but needs protection from frost.

Below: **Paeonia suffruticosa**
These stunning 15cm/6in blooms are white with a maroon-purple blotch at the base of each petal. The plant needs some shade.

Philadelphus coronarius 'Aureus'

(Golden-leaved mock orange)

- **Full sun**
- **Any good garden soil**
- **Summer flowering**

This hardy deciduous shrub is one of the sweetest scented shrubs. 'Aureus' is the golden-leaved cultivar; in spring the foliage is a bright golden-yellow, but it becomes duller after midsummer. The oval lance-shaped leaves are 4-8cm/1.6-3.2in long, and slightly toothed. The creamy-white sweetly scented flowers which appear in summer make this golden beauty an ideal fragrant shrub.

It rarely grows to more than 2.7m/9ft, so it is ideal for the small or medium-sized garden. Do not provide too rich a soil, and it will tolerate chalk soils; it is a good shrub for growing in coastal areas. As the flowers are produced on the previous year's shoots, pruning should be carried out as soon as the flowers are over; cut back old flowering wood to strong new growths.

Propagate by hardwood cuttings in autumn, and insert out of doors.

Take care
Remove old worn-out shoots from time to time.

Right: **Philadelphus 'Manteau d'Hermine'**
This is one of several excellent hybrids. It bears double or triple creamy-white flowers during the summer months which scent the whole garden. It grows to about 1m/39in tall.

Below right: **Philadelphus 'Virginal'**
A singularly beautiful hybrid with double or semi-double white cup-shaped blooms. It has a unique fragrance and grows up to 2.5m/8ft tall, making it suitable for a medium-sized plot.

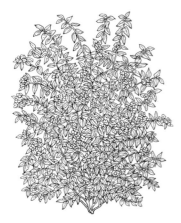

Philadelphus modern hybrids
(Mock orange)
- **Full sun**
- **Any good garden soil**
- **Summer flowering**

Over the years many beautiful hybrid varieties of philadelphus have been raised and introduced. The following are worthy of space in a small or medium-sized garden. 'Belle Etoile' has fragrant white flowers with a reddish blotch in the centre of each flower; it grows to a height of 1.5-2m/5-6.5ft. 'Sybille' has large saucer-shaped fragrant flowers which are up to 5cm/2in wide, borne singly or in twos or threes; the blooms are purplish-white at the base of each petal, with sea-green foliage, and the shrub is 1.2-2m/4-6.5ft tall. A third beauty is the double or semi-double white cup-shaped fragrant 'Virginal', which reaches 2-2.5m/6.5-8ft tall. The compact 'Manteau d'Hermine', with creamy-white fragrant flowers borne usually in threes, grows to about 1m/39in tall.

The general care and cultivation, pruning and propagation of all these varieties are exactly the same as for *P. coronarius* 'Aureus'.

Take care
Remove old stems as necessary.

Left: **Potentilla 'Elizabeth'**
This shrubby potentilla puts on a magnificent show of colour from late spring until early autumn. A hardy dependable plant for sun or partial shade and in any soil.

Potentilla 'Elizabeth'
(Cinquefoil)
- **Sun or partial shade**
- **Any good soil**
- **Flowers from late spring to early autumn**

The shrubby potentillas are hardy and free-flowering; there are many varieties and hybrids. 'Elizabeth' is probably a hybrid between *P. arbuscula* and *P. dahurica* var. *veitchii*. Originally it was grown under the species *P. arbuscula*. This deciduous dome-shaped bush is about 1m/39in high, and as much in width; from late spring to early autumn it is adorned with large rich primrose-yellow strawberry-like flowers up to 4cm/1.6in in diameter. Today there are many to choose from: 'Katherine Dykes' has primrose-yellow flowers; 'Red Ace' has pale yellow flowers and is only 50cm/20in high.

They thrive in any good garden soil, and do well in full sun, but also tolerate partial shade. Propagate by seeds in late winter, or by half-ripe cuttings in late summer.

Take care
Remove worn-out stems down to ground level.

Prunus laurocerasus 'Otto Luyken'
- **Sun or dappled shade**
- **Good fertile soil; not chalk soils**
- **Spring flowering**

A fine low-growing hardy evergreen 1-1.2m/3.3-4ft tall with a spread of (eventually) 2.1-2.7m/7-9ft. It has glossy deep green leathery foliage, the leaves almost 2.5cm/1in wide, and pointed at either end; they are thickly set on ascending branches, which grow at a semi-erect angle from the ground. This free-flowering variety produces vertical terminal racemes of white flowers. It is an outstanding evergreen especially for small or medium-sized gardens, and it is ideal as a ground cover shrub.

Normally pruning will not be necessary, but if it has to be done, choose the spring or the early part of the summer.

Propagate by hardwood cuttings during the summer inserted out of doors in a border facing away from the sun.

Take care
Give room to spread naturally.

Above: **Prunus laurocerasus 'Otto Luyken'**
Extemely useful as ground cover, this low-growing evergreen shrub bears abundant terminal flower clusters in spring. It will flourish in the shade of trees.

Right: **Prunus lusitanica**
Here grown as a standard tree, the Portugal laurel can also form a dense bush. It will thrive in any type of soil, including chalk, and looks best when grown as a specimen plant.

Prunus lusitanica

(Portugal laurel)
- **Sun or dappled shade**
- **Warm and well-drained soil**
- **Early summer flowering and foliage**

This handsome evergreen shrub needs to be grown as an isolated specimen where its rich green glossy foliage can be appreciated. In early summer it produces a mass of long slender racemes of dull white flowers, followed later by a profusion of small purple cherries. From time to time specimens are trained so that they have a broad squat head of foliage on a short stem; old specimens eventually have a stout trunk. Bushes or standard trees can be anything from 3-4.5m/10-15ft tall, with a spread of 4.5m/15ft or even wider.

When pruning is needed, this should be done in spring or early summer. The cultivar 'Variegata' has leaves margined with white, and in winter the foliage is often flushed with pink. A large specimen can grow 1.5-2m/5-6ft tall, and somewhat wider.

Propagate by hardwood cuttings in autumn, inserted out of doors.

Take care
Cut out any shoots that have silver leaf, and treat wounds with a fungicidal pruning paint.

Prunus 'Sato Zakura'

(Japanese cherries)
- Full sun
- Any well-drained soil
- Spring flowering

The following two Japanese cherries are especially suitable for small and medium-sized gardens. The erect *Prunus* 'Amanogawa' is a columnar tree which can grow up to 5m/16.4ft tall. At first the young foliage is yellowish, before turning green; in early to mid-spring this tree is bedecked with fragrant semi-double soft pink flowers, and in the autumn its coloured foliage provides a dazzling display.

Where an attractive pendulous tree is wanted, grow 'Cheal's Weeping'. This small tree has attractive arching branches covered with deep pink double flowers. The young leaves are bronze-green, changing later to a glossy green; it is also colourful in autumn. Mature specimens can be 4.5m/15ft or taller. To encourage this cherry to flower, pinch out the tips of all lateral shoots when they are 1-1.2m/39in-4ft long. Propagate both these cherries by budding in the summer, or by grafting in the early part of the spring.

Take care
Remove unwanted shoots which appear below the graft union.

Prunus subhirtella 'Pendula'

(Weeping spring cherry)
- Full sun
- Any fertile, neutral soil
- Spring flowering

P. subhirtella 'Pendula' is an excellent pendulous tree which is eminently suitable for a small or medium-sized garden, as it reaches only 3.6-5.55m/12-18ft in height with a spread of approximately 6m/20ft. The tiny pale pink blossoms are abundantly produced in the springtime on the base branches of this deciduous weeping tree.

Another form of *P. subhirtella* is the cultivar 'Autumnalis', which grows to 5-6m/16.4-20ft tall, producing almond-scented semi-double white flowers from the late autumn throughout the winter until the early springtime. It develops into a wide-branched small tree with a dense twiggy crown. The autumn apricot tints are particularly attractive.

No regular pruning is necessary where this tree is concerned. It can be propagated by budding in the summer, or, alternatively, by grafting on to appropriate stocks during the spring.

Take care
Remove any suckers which might arise from the stocks.

Ribes sanguineum 'Pulborough Scarlet'

(Flowering currant)
- Sunny position
- Any good garden soil
- Spring flowering

This deciduous spring-flowering shrub has produced a number of cultivars. 'Pulborough Scarlet' has deep red flowers. These make a pleasing contrast to the rich moss-green foliage as it unfolds at the time of flowering. Sprays of 20 to 30 flowers are borne on long wand-like growths.

This vigorous shrub reaches a height of 2-2.5m/6.5-8ft or higher, and as much in width. The palmately three- to five-lobed leaves have a heart-shaped base 5-10cm/2-4in wide but less in length. This attractive shrub is disliked by some people because of the pungent smell of its flowers and foliage.

Prune by removing an occasional old branch or a few side shoots after the flowering period has passed.

Propagate by hardwood cuttings, in the autumn or winter.

Take care
It is important to allow enough room for this shrub to expand as it can grow up to 2.5m/8ft in width.

Far left: **Prunus 'Cheal's Weeping'**
A graceful Japanese cherry adorned with double pink flowers in spring. In terms of its eventual size it is perfect for small gardens.

Left: **Prunus subhirtella 'Pendula'**
Spring sunshine playing on these delicate pale pink flowers creates a superb spectacle in the spring months.

Above: **Ribes sanguineum**
Where space permits, this vigorous spring-flowering shrub will grow into a large bush. This shrub has a distinctive aroma.

43

Left: **Robinia pseudoacacia 'Frisia'**
The golden-yellow pinnate foliage and graceful form of this medium-sized tree provide interest from spring through to autumn. It is quite suitable for smaller gardens.

Robinia pseudoacacia 'Frisia'

(Common acacia, False acacia, Black locust, Yellow locust)
● **Full sun**
● **Any well-drained soil**
● **Coloured foliage from spring to autumn**

This species will grow into a fairly large tree, which is often seen in industrial areas. The cultivar called 'Frisia' has become very popular, partly because it makes a small to medium-sized tree and is therefore suited to a small or medium-sized garden. It has rich golden-yellow pinnate foliage that creates a superb splash of colour from spring through to autumn. Trees can be anything from 6-8m/20-26ft high. The thorns on young growths are red, which, with the young golden-yellow foliage, makes a striking sight.

Any pruning that is necessary should be carried out during mid- or late summer, as there is then less chance of the tree bleeding. Where large wounds are left, treat them with a suitable tree paint.

Propagate by grafting 'Frisia' on to stocks of *R. pseudoacacia* in spring out of doors.

Take care
Treat wounds with a tree paint.

Left: **Rosa rugosa 'Frau Dagmar Hastrup'**
*Suited to smaller spaces, this makes an ideal
hedge due to its prickly and dense growing habit.
Perpetual flowering is followed by large red hips.*

Below: **Rubus Tridel 'Benenden'**
*These elegant and fragrant flowers, up to
8cm/3.2in across, appear on arching stems in
the late spring. A vigorous shrub.*

Rosa rugosa 'Frau Dagmar Hastrup'
(Rose)
● **Sun, but tolerates shade**
● **Most soils; avoid chalk or clay**
● **Perpetual flowering**

R. rugosa 'Frau Dagmar Hastrup' is particularly
suitable for the small garden. Like other rugosas
it has thick dark green wrinkled foliage. The fairly
large rose-pink flowers have a conspicuous
centre of creamy-yellow stamens; the buds are a
rich deep pink. The beautiful blooms are
moderately scented and continuously produced.
The bush has a compact habit, reaching 1.5m/5ft
tall and 1.2m/4ft wide. The foliage has splendid
autumn colouring, and from summer into autumn
there are rich crimson tomato-shaped hips,
larger than most. Rugosas are very prickly.

Very little pruning is needed; but if bushes
become ungainly, they can be cut back in spring.

Propagate by cuttings 23cm/9in long, with a
heel or cut just below a bud, in autumn or early
winter; or remove suckers in autumn.

Take care
Do not over-prune except when rejuvenation is
needed.

Rubus Tridel 'Benenden'
● **Sun or partial shade**
● **Ordinary well-drained loamy or chalk soil**
● **Late spring flowering**

This deciduous hardy flowering shrub is a hybrid
between *Rubus trilobus* and *Rubus deliciosus*
giving it a group name of Tridel, whereas the
clone name is 'Benenden'. It has dark green
leaves with three to five lobes. This vigorous
shrub of the bramble family has spineless stems
with peeling bark. The tall arching branches
reach a height of approximately 2.5-3m/8-10ft. In
the late spring the shrub produces many single
pure white scented flowers, 6-8cm/2.3-3.2in
across, each flower with a central boss of
golden-yellow stamens.

Pruning consists of cutting out the oldest wood
after flowering, to encourage an annual supply of
new growth from the base; this will produce
flowers in the following year. Do not cut out too
much old wood.

Propagate by layering in spring, even though
they may take 12 months to root.

Take care
Encourage young growths to develop from the
base of the shrub.

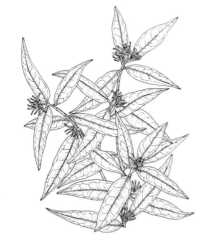

Sarcococca humilis

(Sweet box)

- Tolerates heavy shade
- Any moist fertile soil
- Flowers in late winter or early spring

This shrub is in no way related to the *Buxus* genus. It is a neat dwarf evergreen tufted shrub, densely branched and as a rule not more than 30-60cm/1-2ft high. It has a suckering habit, not unlike butcher's broom, and is excellent for planting in groups as a ground cover plant. The narrow oval willow-like foliage is glossy green above but paler beneath; the leaves are 3-8cm/1.2-3.2in long, and tapered at the apex. The axillary fragrant flowers are white with pink anthers, and are usually produced in spring, though at times they are to be found blooming in autumn or winter. The flowers are followed by blue-black berries.

No pruning is required, apart from the removal of old stems and any dead growth; do this after flowering has finished.

Propagate by division in the spring or by hardwood cuttings in the autumn inserted in an unheated frame.

Take care
Remove old and worn-out stems after flowering is finished.

Spiraea

- Sunny position
- Any good garden soil
- Spring flowering

When dealing with spiraeas the problem is which to include; the four described here are hardy deciduous shrubs that flower in the spring. All are easily grown in any good garden soil, including chalk or lime soils.

The spring-flowering *S. x arguta* is a graceful branching shrub about 1.5-2m/5-6.5ft high, with slender twiggy growth, and dainty pure white flowers produced in clusters on arching sprays of bloom. *S. media* is an erect shrub up to 1.2-2m/4-6.5ft tall that bears long-stalked racemes of white flowers. *S. prunifolia* is the same height as *S. media*; the double white flowers in rosette-like clusters are borne along arching stems. Lastly, the pale green *S. thunbergii* has pure white flowers produced on wiry leafless stems in clusters of two to five; the shrub is approximately 90cm-1.5m/3-5ft tall.

Once flowering has finished, remove old flowering shoots and shorten any long shoots. Propagate this shrub by half-ripe cuttings taken in the summer.

Take care
Keep bushes shapely.

Viburnum x bodnantense

- Sunny position
- Any good fertile soil
- Flowers in autumn and winter

This vigorous deciduous flowering shrub is a hybrid between *V. farreri (V. fragrans)* and *V. grandiflorum*. It appears to sulk for a few years at first, but once established there is no holding it. This is one of the finest and most frost-resistant winter flowering shrubs available.

The hybrid named 'Dawn' is the form most commonly seen in cultivation. It has buds that are first rose-red, and then they open into clusters of sweetly fragrant rose-tinted white flowers on the naked branches, followed by deep green foliage with red stalks. The height of this hybrid is approximately 2.5-3m/8-10ft, and sometimes can be more than this.

When pruning is needed, remove complete old or weak branches at ground level; this will encourage new growth to develop from the base of the plant.

Propagate by layering; rooted branches often layer naturally, otherwise layers can be put down during early summer.

Take care
Give this viburnum as much space as possible to spread itself.

Bottom left: **Sarcococca humilis**
Grow this evergreen shrub as ground cover in shady situations. It forms a dense bush only 60cm/2ft high. The fragrant white flowers appear in late winter and early spring.

Right: **Spiraea thunbergii**
This spring-flowering deciduous shrub grows quickly in any good soil to a height of about 1.5m/5ft. Prune it after flowering to keep the bush shapely and vigorous.

Below: **Viburnum** x **bodnantense**
These sweetly scented rose-pink flowers are produced during the autumn and winter. They are remarkably frost-resistant. Plant this shrub in an open and sunny position in any fertile soil.

Left: **Viburnum plicatum 'Mariesii'**
The early summer flowers resemble Lacecap hydrangeas. The branches, wherever possible, should be given room to spread horizontally.

Viburnum plicatum 'Mariesii'
- Prefers partial shade
- Any moist fertile soil
- Flowers in late spring and early summer

This deciduous horizontal-branched flowering shrub seems happier with some shade, rather than in full sun. The oval-pointed leaves are toothed except at the base, 5-10cm/2-4in long, up to 6.5cm/2.5in wide, dull dark green above, pale greyish beneath, and slightly downy. Bushes can be 1.5-3m/5-10ft high, and wider, so this shrub must be given room to spread. The large inflorescences have ray flowers about 4.5cm/1.8in wide with the pinhead fertile flowers in the centre, held on stalks about 6.5cm/2.5in long. The foliage in autumn turns to dull crimson or purplish-red.

No regular pruning is needed for this shrub. Propagate by summer layering, or by half-ripe cuttings of the current year's growth taken during the summer months.

Take care
If possible, allow this lovely shrub plenty of room to stretch itself.

Viburnum tinus
(Laurustinus)
- Full sun or partial shade
- Any good garden soil, including chalk
- Winter and spring flowers

An evergreen flowering shrub that makes a dense rounded bush. The opposite leaves, dark glossy green above and paler beneath, are borne on red stalks; the main shoots are red above, green beneath and warted. At the ends of the leafy shoots are terminal flower clusters 5-10cm/2-4in across. The greeny buds are tinged with mauvy-pink before opening white in winter and spring, followed by deep blue fruits that become black. Bushes reach 2-3.6m/6.5-12ft.

Laurustinus does well on chalk or non-chalk soils and is excellent in coastal areas. Prune bushes that have grown out of hand or are frost damaged by cutting them hard back to the oldest wood near ground level in late spring.

Propagate by seed sown in late winter, or by half-ripe heel cuttings from early to late summer.

Take care
Allow to grow naturally.

Above: **Viburnum tinus**
This evergreen easy-care shrub blooms during the winter and early spring. The white flowers are followed by blue fruits that then turn black.

Right: **Weigela 'Bristol Ruby'**
*This is one of several hybrids that provide
trouble-free summer colour in the garden. All
enjoy a rich moist soil and a sunny location.
Prune after flowering each year.*

Weigela hybrids
● **Full sun**
● **Rich fertile soil, including chalk**
● **Summer flowering**

These are trouble-free deciduous flowering
shrubs of which there are a number of attractive
hybrids. The flowers are similar to those of
honeysuckle except that all are scentless.
Hybrids that are usually available include: 'Abel
Carrière', a deep carmine with a yellow throat,
and a strong grower that can be 2m by 2m/6.5ft
by 6.5ft; 'Bristol Ruby', a bright ruby-red with
almost black buds, fairly upright in habit, 2m by
1.5m/6.5ft by 5ft; 'Candida', pure white with
bright green foliage, 2m by 2m/6.5ft by 6.5ft or
even wider; and 'Newport Red', bright red.

They are all easily grown, provided they have
rich soil with ample moisture at their roots. Prune
regularly as soon as they have finished flowering,
and then remove old flowering side branches.
Overgrown bushes can be cut hard back in
spring.

Propagate by hardwood cuttings in autumn,
inserted out of doors.

Take care
Prune annually after flowering.

Part Two: Conifers

Introduction

I wish there was a simple answer to the question: 'What are conifers?' but there is not. Some are cone-bearers, such as the pines; others have berries, such as the yews; and others have fruit-like seed cases. Some are evergreen, but not all. They all have resinous glands, but some other trees also produce resin. Some conifers have needle-like foliage, but others have flat leaves, and some are scale-like. The main characteristic in common is the strong central stem from which other branches radiate, but in some of the dwarf and prostrate varieties this is difficult to see. Without going into a more complex biological explanation and using very technical language it is difficult to explain what conifers are. Let us say that the term includes the pines, firs, cupressus, cedars, larches and junipers, with the addition of a few other minor groups.

In the wild most conifers make upright trees with the shape of a column, cone, or pyramid. Due to local conditions, such as desert, mountain or arctic areas where there is little nutrition, harsh temperatures and constricted root areas, a few species have become dwarfed. From these few hundred wild plants have been developed the thousands of cultivated trees and shrubs with a wide variety of forms and colours. The expert grower searches out a plant malformation, such as unusually pale colour, a cluster of tight growth, or a branch that tries to grow in the wrong direction. This is removed and used to propagate more plants of the same habit through cuttings. The demand for smaller plants to fit into the tiny gardens that are available with new housing developments today means that there is a ready market for slow-growing and dwarf conifers.

With the ever-increasing need for good-looking, low-maintenance gardens, more gardeners are turning to conifers to provide a simple answer, interplanted with shrubs or heathers and used as ground cover. Conifers give an interesting planting with no lawn to mow or edges to trim and requiring very little care, no flowers to plant and lift as the season demands but a pleasant garden that looks good in all seasons.

Most conifers are easy to grow with little maintenance during the year: there are few leaves to sweep up and negligible pruning; pests and diseases are minimal; and provided the hardier varieties are grown there is little trouble from drought, wind or cold once the plants are established.

Where to plant conifers

The garden designer usually relies on conifers to provide the backbone of the planting plan; they provide a basic structure that is there all the year, with tall, round or flat shapes of a constant colour and form around which to add other plants and develop seasonal changes of colour and pattern. In fact, there are a few gardeners who will grow *only* evergreen trees and shrubs, because they find bare trunks and twigs, dead flowers and brown leaves depressing. But whatever image one has of the ideal garden, it should certainly contain at least a few conifers as a contrast to other plants.

Small and dwarf conifers fit into a rockery and mix with other rockery plants, providing a vertical shape or horizontal accent that can make a necessary division between areas. Their distinctive form also acts as a fine contrast in a bed of heathers, the extra height making the bed more interesting and exciting to look at. The conifers usually remain a fairly constant colour, apart from a small number that sprout new growth in the spring; this can produce delightful fresh pale colours, and make candles, tassels or spots of interest on the plant.

The growth is usually slow, and the dwarf and slow-growing conifers will remain in scale with their surroundings for many years, although they may need replacing after twenty years or so, when they may begin to spread over other garden plantings. Some thrive in containers or sink gardens, where their roots are constricted and their size remains fairly constant.

Large conifers come into their own as specimen plants in a border or set into the lawn, where they have plenty of space to spread and grow to their full height. It is wise to check on the ultimate height and age when choosing, as this can determine where to put them. Some take several centuries to mature and it could be that the house will disappear before the tree is fully grown.

Buying conifers

When you buy conifers you will find that there are different ways in which they have been prepared. At first sight the difference is in the way the plant has been grown; it may be in a pot, or the roots may be wrapped up in hessian or polythene, and sometimes the roots are bare and just bundled up in some plastic. If you go to a reputable nursery there is usually a choice between the pot- or container-grown plant and one that has been grown in a nursery bed, lifted and the generous rootball wrapped to keep it moist. The container plant can be moved and planted at any time of year with little disturbance to the roots; this plant is more expensive than one with wrapped roots, which is normally for sale only in autumn or spring, when the plant is dormant and soil conditions are suitable. The cheapest plants are seedlings that are usually bundled together and sold primarily for hedging, and these have the minimum of soil around the roots; these give the highest rate of failure, but for anyone with a great deal of hedging to plant, this could be the only way to afford it.

When buying, choose a plant with a bright healthy appearance, and strong growth to the lower parts. The soil should fill the width of the pot or container and look as if it has been in this state for some time. Freshly moved soil suggests that the plant has been lifted out of a nursery bed and popped into a pot to command a higher price. Avoid plants that look tired, with the leaves drooping or browning, and with a rootball that is loose in the container. If it is sold as a rootball plant in hessian, make sure that the ball is moist and not dried up. Look for signs of insect attack and eggs left on the undersides of leaves; on stems and leaves watch for moulds, black spots and rusty markings and choose your conifers from those that are free of these.

Sometimes plants are offered with a marked difference in prices for similar plants, and this could be due to the nature of the propagation method. The cheapest way to grow plants is by seed; this is simply sown and the resulting seedlings are grown on to form saleable specimens. But some species either have no seed (being male plants) or the seed, if sown, will not grow true but will revert back to the original parent whose size and colour can vary widely; these species are usually grown from cuttings. Shoots are cut off the parent plant, one end is inserted into a cuttings mixture that will encourage root growth, and the new plants are kept in a protected area for two or three years before being sold to the customer.

Certain cultivars are not very good when grown from cuttings, because their roots are poor and they can revert to a different colour or form; in this case, cuttings are taken and grafted on to a rootstock. This entails taking a cutting and slicing a clean angle on the stem; the rootstock is a small seedling with all its foliage removed and a similar angle cut on its stem. The two angles are put together and bound up to allow the sap to flow between the two parts. This union will gradually join up, often making a slight swelling on the stem. The plant is then grown on for up to four years to ensure that the union is satisfactory, before the plant is put on sale.

These grafted plants are the most labour-intensive, and understandably more expensive. When you examine your potential purchase do look at the stem for the tell-tale bulge that shows it was propagated from a graft; this is a sign of a good plant, particularly with the named varieties of *Abies*, *Picea* and *Pinus*.

The middle-priced plants grown from cuttings are usually smooth-stemmed and are named varieties. The cheapest plants are those that grow well in the wild. Of course there are exceptions, such as plants that are very rare, or whose seed has to be brought great distances, and in some instances the seed is very sparse and consequently expensive.

Planting conifers

First it is important to choose the right place for your plant: an open site with the recommended amount of sun or shade, protection from winds and cold, the right type of soil with the correct level of moisture, and space to grow. Some places

Right: **Abies concolor 'Glauca Compacta'**
A highly recommended conifer for rockeries, containers or as a lawn specimen – wherever its attractive foliage can be seen to best advantage.

used for planting are most unsuitable. One house near where I am writing has a front garden that is 2m/6.5ft from front door to gate, but squeezed into a narrow border along the path is a line of six *Cupressocyparis leylandii* to form a hedge. In three years they have grown over 1.8m/6ft without any pruning or check on their growth, and if left to their own devices they will swamp the whole garden and cut off daylight from the front of the house completely.

The soil is important and can make the plant stunted or rampant. For most a soil that is in good heart, neither too acid nor too alkaline, moist but well drained is adequate. Some are particular about the amount of moisture, others are in need of protection from drought, and others require a deep soil rich in nutrients. Whichever soil you have, it is possible to improve the balance to suit most conifers. Generally the addition of peat, leaf-mould and bonemeal will help light sandy soils to retain more moisture, and if added to heavy clay soils they will increase the drainage and open the texture of the clay to enable plants to establish their roots.

If you have an acid soil that needs to be neutralized, the application of lime is beneficial. For alkaline soils the answer is plenty of wet peat, old pine needles, leaf-mould and a good dose of chelates of iron, usually sold as sequestrene. For the gardener who wants an easy life without the effort of soil conditioning it is simpler to choose a plant that will fit the soil, rather than making the soil fit the plant.

It is important to dig a hole bigger than the rootball. Weeds should be carefully removed, and the soil dug over to break it up to improve drainage; this is particularly important on clay soils. Fill the hole with water and let it drain away. Remove the container from the plant or take off the wrapping around the rootball, gently tease out the surface of the rootball to expose some of the fine hair-like roots, and place the ball in the hole. The soil level should be higher than the soil mark on the plant's stem, to encourage root growth and to help stabilize the whole plant. Fill in the hole, treading the soil down well to make sure that there are no air pockets around the roots. Then give another good dose of water, using a fine rose in order not to wash away the soil.

During the first year water the plant whenever the soil becomes dry: this includes wetting the foliage when there are drying winds. A layer of peat, pulverized bark or compost spread over the root area will help the plant to retain moisture during droughts. In a rock garden this mulching could look wrong, and a generous layer of stone chips which matches the surrounding area will make a good substitute.

Until the plant has established itself, it is wise to keep at least 30cm/1ft of soil around each conifer clear of weeds, to allow the plant to breathe. This is particularly important with slow-growing dwarf varieties, which can easily be overwhelmed and choked by other more vigorous plants growing close by.

How healthy are conifers?
The health of conifers is normally quite good. There is a greater danger from drought, excess moisture and wrong soil conditions than from pests and diseases. They do occur, however, and normally they can be controlled with a spray of pesticide and fungicide. Forestry areas have

Below: **Chamaecyparis pisifera 'Filifera Aurea'**
The golden thread-like foliage of this specimen makes it ideal as a focal point in the garden. In ten years it grows to a height of 1m/39in.

problems when deer and rabbits cause damage, but unless you live in a very rural area where these animals roam freely, they can be ignored.

When using chemicals, make sure that you read the instructions properly and follow them exactly. Most garden chemicals have to pass a very stringent test for danger to the environment, but if the dilution, timing and method of application are not followed, the wrong insects can be killed, soil and plants spoilt, and your health endangered. There are newer, improved chemicals arriving on the market all the time and it is wise to check to find out what old products have been superseded by better ones.

Do conifers need pruning?
On the whole conifers need very little pruning. In fact, for some it is not recommended at all, as it can cause the cut branch to die back even further. Some conifers need just a little trimming to tidy their shape, but others are grown as hedges and require regular cutting to keep the hedge neat. The topiary enthusiast can train and clip conifers into the most extraordinary shapes, but use only plants that will stand this treatment, such as yew.

Most conifers have their own particular form: some are column-like, others conical, some pyramidal; there are weeping forms, trailing or prostrate varieties, or even semi-prostrate ones where some branches try to grow upwards; and there are bun shapes and mound-forming plants. With these different types it is better to allow their forms to grow naturally.

Why have I selected these conifers?
This is a personal selection to give a wide coverage of plants and their forms and foliage colours. With only space for a limited number of conifers from thousands, there are bound to be omissions, and to readers who find that their particular favourite is missing I extend my apologies. I have chosen plants that are commercially available: many will be for sale at the local garden centre, but for some you will need to write or go to a specialist grower who stocks the rarer specimens. Within these constraints, I hope I have managed a balance of sorts.

The use of Latin names is important because it is an international system. Common names vary from district to district and from country to country, and what is a white pine to one person is something completely different to another. It is easy to mix up firs and pines, and also to think that all plants with scale-like leaves are cupressus. The most usual common names are given after the Latin name and indexed separately at the back of the book.

David Papworth

A-Z Index by Latin Name

Above: **Picea Abies 'Little Gem'**
An ideal subject for a rockery, or a sink or scree garden, this plant makes a round dwarf bush and will only grow to a height of 30cm/1ft over the first ten years of its life.

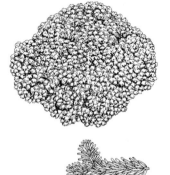

Abies balsamea 'Hudsonia'

(Balsam fir)
- **Provide shelter when young**
- **Deep moist soil**
- **Slow-growing small bush**

This variety forms a dwarf shrub up to 30cm/1ft tall in ten years, but can reach 75cm/30in in 30 years. Branches and foliage form a dense, compact bush with a flattish top, spreading to almost 1m/39in wide. In winter it has resinous buds; in spring these open and expose soft flat grey leaves that turn to mid-green as they mature during the summer.

This is an ideal rockery plant as it remains in scale with other rockery species. The cylindrical cones grow on the upper sides of the branches. They open and break up when the seed is ripe.

Plant the seeds during late winter for extra stock. Avoid extremes of soil such as boggy situations, pure sand or chalk; but grow in a deep moist well-drained soil. Place in an area protected against hard frost, which can damage the young shoots. This variety is normally pest- and disease-free.

Take care
Avoid frost on young shoots

Abies concolor 'Glauca Compacta'

(Colorado white fir)
- **Stands heat and dry conditions**
- **Avoid chalky soils**
- **Slow-growing small bush**

This dwarf shrub from America is one of the best conifers for the rock garden, or even as a specimen for a lawn or a container. It has silver-blue foliage that grows in a slightly irregular form, giving it an attractive character. It can take up to 25 years to reach 75cm/30in tall, with a spread of just over 1m/39in. It prefers a deep moist soil but will tolerate hot and dry conditions; avoid a chalky soil. The winter buds are large and resinous, and open in spring to pale hairless clusters of leaves. The cones, almost 25cm/10in long, are pale green when young but turn purple as they mature.

This shrub can be grown from seed, but the plant may vary in colour; it is normally propagated by grafting the right shade of leaf on to a dwarf rootstock. The plants are generally free from pests and diseases.

Take care
Avoid waterlogged sites.

Above: **Abies concolor 'Glauca Compacta'**
This dwarf shrub has silver-blue foliage and a compact habit. It will tolerate hot, dry conditions but chalky soil should be avoided.

Right: **Abies koreana 'Nana'**
A dwarf Korean fir which is prized for its prolific purple cones and its attractive new growth during the spring months.

Abies koreana

(Korean fir)
● **Thrives in humid conditions**
● **Deep moist soil**
● **Slow-growing small tree**

This small neat slow-growing tree is very popular for its dark green leaves; for its prolific violet-purple cones, just over 5cm/2in long; and for its slow growth. Used on rockeries or in a container, it will take over ten years to reach 3m/10ft, but where there is unrestricted space it may eventually reach 10m/33ft. The tree has a regular tapering shape. In spring, the new silvery-grey leaves contrast with the darker blue-green mature growth. The cones are borne on the upper side of the branches and appear on quite young specimens. There are two dwarf-growing varieties, 'Compact Dwarf' and 'Nana', both suitable for rockeries.

When the seeds ripen they can be sown in a seed compost in the early spring and left for two or three years before planting into their final positions. Grow this plant in a deep moist soil that is free from chalk. The tree is both pest- and disease-free.

Take care
Avoid boggy soil conditions.

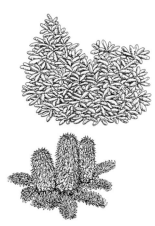

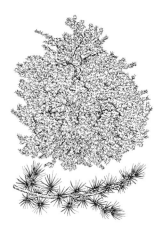

Abies lasiocarpa arizonica
(Cork fir)
- Prefers humid conditions
- Deep moist soil
- Slow-growing medium tree

This medium-sized tree has thick corky bark, and its distinctive winter buds are white and resinous. It will reach 18m/59ft tall where conditions are good, but the average plant reaches half this size. The leaves are silvery-grey; the smallish cones, which are 7.5cm/3in long, are purple when young.

When the cones start to break up, collect the seed and sow in a seed compost in early spring. Allow the seedlings to grow on in a seed bed for over two years before planting out in their permanent positions. Plant this tree in a deep moist soil that is free or almost free from lime. A slow-growing dwarf cultivar, 'Compacta', has blue-grey foliage, and may take ten years to reach 70cm/28in.

Watch for white waxy wool on the leaves and branches, caused by adelgids; spray with malathion in late spring to control an attack. If the stems start to die back, spray the tree with a fungicide to deter fungus.

Take care
Avoid a waterlogged site.

Abies procera 'Glauca Prostrata'
(Noble fir)
- Suits most situations
- Avoid chalky soil
- Slow-growing low bush

This low-growing bush has parents that can reach 60m/197ft and originates in the western United States. The dwarf cultivar makes a fine specimen for the rockery or border. The blue-green leaves have a fine curled form, and the compact branches give it an interesting shape. The cones are brown, up to 25cm/10in long, with downward-pointing green bracts that almost cover the cone.

It is best grown from grafted cuttings in order to keep a dwarf variety. These should be kept in a nursery bed for a few years before planting out in their final situation. Grow in a deep, moist but well-drained acid soil. If the leading shoot starts to grow vigorously it should be pruned in spring to keep a low shape.

Spray with malathion to keep the sap-sucking adelgids from attacking the plant, and use a fungicide to prevent fungal attack.

Take care
Watch out for a vigorous leader and then prune back.

Cedrus libani 'Nana'
(Dwarf Lebanon cedar)
- Prefers a warm dry place
- Well-drained garden soil
- Slow-growing small bush

The original dwarf varieties were probably found growing in restricted pockets of soil. These have been cultivated and now there are various dwarf forms known as 'Nana', all fairly similar with a bushy shape, slow-growing and dense. They will reach a height of about 1m/39in with a similar spread, but with a growth rate of around 2.5cm/1in a year they take some time to reach full size. The small needles are dark or greyish-green. A little pruning is needed to keep the form; remove some branches to prevent overcrowding. This is an ideal bush for growing in rockeries, sink gardens, containers or simply in the garden border.

Graft these plants a minimum of three years before planting out into their final positions, to make sure that the graft is firmly established. Plant in a soil enriched with peat, leaf-mould and bonemeal, and ensure it is kept weed-free for the first few years.

Take care
Keep these plants in shape with careful pruning during the autumn months.

Bottom far left: **Abies lasiocarpa arizonica**
This distinctive slow-growing conifer has a fine colour and a dwarf habit, making it ideal for planting in rockeries and mixed borders.

Bottom left: **Abies procera 'Glauca Prostrata'**
A magnificent cluster of large cones borne amid fresh spring growth. This plant will thrive in most situations but chalky soils should be avoided.

Below: **Cedrus libani 'Nana'**
This dwarf variety of the Cedar of Lebanon develops slowly into a dense bush. Prune it carefully in the autumn to keep it looking tidy.

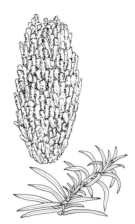

Cephalotaxus harringtonia 'Fastigiata'
(Upright Japanese plumyew)
- Grows in shade
- Prefers chalky soil
- Slow-growing small tree

Originating probably in China but cultivated for several centuries in Japan, this small tree has an upright form with the appearance of a large-leaved variety of *Taxus baccata* 'Fastigiata', the Irish yew. Its very dark green leaves, up to 6.4cm/2.5in long, are arranged around the vertical stems. The tree is slow-growing to start with; it will grow to 1.5m/5ft in ten years and eventually will reach 5m/16.4ft. There are male and female trees, and the 2.5cm/1in cones appear on females.

Seeds can be sown in a seed compost in autumn; plant out the seedlings in a nursery bed when they are about 7.5cm/3in tall, and grow on for two or three years before planting them out in their final situations. This tree will grow in shade even under other trees.

This variety may be attacked by scale insects, which should be sprayed with malathion.

Take care
Avoid waterlogged soil.

Left: **Cephalotaxus harringtonia 'Fastigiata'**
This slow-growing small tree forms a neat upright shape. It is useful in that it will grow happily in shady situations.

Chamaecyparis lawsoniana 'Aurea Densa'

- Open situation
- Ordinary garden soil
- Very slow-growing dwarf bush

The parents of this plant originated in the western USA, but this particular form was raised in England in 1939. The dwarf golden-leaved plant grows to 2m/6.5ft, but will take about 30 years to reach half this height. It is ideal for the rockery, container, sink garden or border, where its densely packed fans of flattened leaves and its regular conical shape will be seen to advantage. It has tiny green cones which are approximately 6mm/0.2in in diameter. These turn brown as they ripen.

The seeds can be sown, but seedlings can vary a lot. It is better to take cuttings, in an equal mix of peat and sand in a cold frame in spring. Transplant them into nursery beds in autumn and grow on for three years before moving to their final situation.

Normally these plants are free from pests and diseases except for honey fungus.

Take care
Keep an area around the young plant free from weeds and other plants.

Above: **Chamaecyparis lawsoniana 'Aurea Densa'**
A dense, slow-growing dwarf cultivar suitable for rockeries and containers. It has flattened leaves and forms a regular conical shape.

Chamaecyparis lawsoniana 'Elwoodii'

- Open or lightly shaded site
- Well-drained garden soil
- Slow-growing bush

Probably one of the best-known cultivars of its family, this is ideal for the small garden or rockery. It is of garden origin from cross-pollination of other cultivars developed from the western United States parents. It has a fine blue-green colour, and a column-like shape with tight neat foliage on an upright branch system. In ten years it can reach 2m/6.5ft tall and 75cm/30in wide; in 20 years it reaches 3m/10ft. It can be made to grow more slowly by lifting it each year and replanting in autumn. The cones are green, changing to brown as they ripen.

The seeds can be sown, but are unlikely to be true to type. Some growers sow plenty of seed and retain only seedlings that show the colour and characteristics of the parent. To obtain a plant true to its parent, cuttings should be taken; after they root, keep them in a nursery bed for three years.

Take care
Prune to keep a single leader for a well-shaped bush.

Left: **Chamaecyparis lawsoniana 'Elwoodii'**
A slow-growing bush with a neat shape, this is a popular plant for very small gardens. It needs an open situation in order to thrive.

Right: **Chamaecyparis lawsoniana**
'Green Globe'
A superb compact conifer with a fine green colour and soft texture. It will grow in either full sun or light shade.

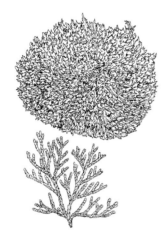

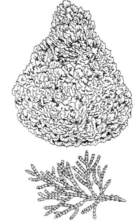

Chamaecyparis lawsoniana 'Green Globe'
- Open or lightly shaded site
- Ordinary well-drained soil
- Slow-growing dwarf bush

This dwarf variety was raised in New Zealand from United States parents. It is the most compact of the dwarf varieties available. Its fine green colour, combined with its globular form, makes it ideal for a rockery, sink garden, container or border where it can be viewed clearly. It will reach 30cm/1ft in ten years, and should eventually reach twice this size. The sprays of leaves give a softer outline than some other miniature forms. The green cones are 6mm/0.2in wide, and turn brown as they ripen.

The seed can be sown, but is unlikely to come true. It is better to take cuttings or to graft on to a dwarf stock. Cuttings should be placed in an equal mixture of peat and sand, and when rooted, transplanted into a nursery bed to grow on for three years. Keep the bed well weeded, and then plant them out in their final situations. Place either in the open or in light shade.

Take care
Keep young plants well weeded.

Chamaecyparis lawsoniana 'Minima Aurea'
- Open situation
- Ordinary garden soil
- Slow-growing dwarf bush

This dwarf rounded bush was raised some 70 years ago. The main difference between this and 'Aurea Densa' is that the forms of foliage are mainly ranged vertically giving it a distinctive texture. Its rounded form is slightly taller than wide, reaching 50cm/20in tall by 40cm/16in wide in ten years, and just over 1m/39in tall by 80cm/32in wide in 30 years. The scale-like leaves are golden-yellow and soft to the touch; they need to be placed in open sunlight to retain their brightness. A rockery situation is ideal for both its colour and its size. The small cones are green, turning to brown when they ripen.

It is best to propagate by taking cuttings, which should be struck in the spring and set in an equal mixture of peat and sand in a cold frame. Plant out the rooted cuttings into a nursery bed in the autumn, grow on for three years, and then plant out.

Take care
Keep the nursery bed weed-free.

Chamaecyparis lawsoniana 'Pembury Blue'
- Open or light shady position
- Well-drained garden soil
- Medium-sized tree

This cultivar, of recent introduction, is probably the bluest of all lawsonianas. Initially it forms an upright bush that develops into a column-like tree 3m/10ft tall by 1m/39in wide, with rather loose-looking fans of foliage; the eventual size is likely to be around 10m/33ft. The vivid silvery-blue leaves are arranged in spiky vertical sprays, the upper branches bearing 6mm/0.2in blue-green cones, which turn brown as they ripen.

It is best to propagate from cuttings. Press them into a mixture of half peat and half sand in spring, and keep them in a cold frame until autumn. They can then be transplanted into a nursery bed for three years, before being planted out in their final situations. Keep the nursery bed free from weeds, or the young plants may be starved of light and nourishment. Place in a good well-drained soil with plenty of peat, leaf-mould and bonemeal added.

Take care
Clear tree of heavy snow.

Above: **Chamaecyparis lawsoniana 'Pembury Blue'**
This beautiful cultivar will grow into a medium-sized tree and makes a fine specimen plant for the average garden. The distinctive foliage is probably the bluest of all the conifers.

Left: **Chamaecyparis lawsoniana 'Minima Aurea'**
An attractive dwarf conifer with striking 'vertical' foliage. This plant needs to be grown in open sunlight if it is to retain its golden colour.

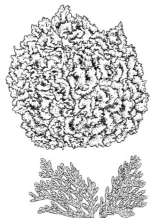

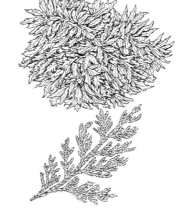

Chamaecyparis lawsoniana 'Pygmaea Argentea'
- Shelter from wind and frost
- Ordinary garden soil
- Very slow-growing dwarf bush

A dwarf variegated bush of rounded shape, also known as 'Backhouse Silver'. Very slow-growing, it will reach only 38cm/15in tall and wide in ten years, and about 1m/39in when fully mature. The foliage is dark green with a dusting of creamy-white around the perimeter of each spray, which looks rather startling, particularly if the plant is placed in a sunny position to keep the blonde edges pale. In winter there is the possibility of some burn on the leaves from frost and wind, but they normally recover in spring. It makes an ideal plant for a rockery, sink garden, or container where it can be seen to advantage.

Propagate from cuttings or by grafting. The cuttings should be struck in spring, transplanted in autumn, and grown on for three years before being planted out.

Generally this bush is free from pests and diseases.

Take care
Young plants may be choked by weeds.

Chamaecyparis lawsoniana 'Tamariscifolia'
- Open site or light shade
- Well-drained garden soil
- Slow-growing compact bush

This plant was raised in England in the 1920s and forms a medium-sized compact bush. It is unkempt when young, as the branches have no distinct form and grow anywhere; but when mature it becomes rounded with a flat top. The branches spread with flat sprays of blue-green leaves, to form a bush about 1.2m/4ft tall and 70cm/28in wide after ten years, and it can eventually reach over 5m/16.4ft in 60 years. The cones, 6mm/0.2in across, are green, gradually turning to brown.

The seeds can be sown, but it is unlikely that seedlings will be true to the parent. It is better to take cuttings, and set them in an equal sand and peat mix. When they have rooted, plant them out into a nursery bed and grow on for three years before transplanting into their final positions. Place in well-drained garden soil enriched with peat, leaf-mould and bonemeal.

Take care
Do not let young plants get choked with weeds.

Chamaecyparis obtusa 'Nana Gracilis'
- Open site or light shade
- Well-drained garden soil
- Slow-growing dwarf bush or small tree

This plant is often sold in nurseries as 'Nana', but it is larger and the sprays of foliage are much flatter. It has the same Japanese origins as 'Nana' and is very popular for the rockery or bonsai. It will reach 1m/39in and 40cm/16in wide in ten years, with an ultimate height of about 2.4m/8ft and a spread of 1m/39in. It is a finely formed plant with distinctive sprays of rich, dark green foliage.

The seeds can be sown and have given rise to some fine small conifers; but to be true to the parent, cuttings should be taken and pressed into a mixture of half peat and half sand. When they have rooted, plant them in nursery beds for three years; keep the ground well weeded. They can then be planted in their final situations where they can be seen to advantage, in ordinary garden soil that is moist but well-drained, with added peat, leaf-mould and bonemeal.

Take care
Keep seedlings weed-free.

Far left: **Chamaecyparis lawsoniana 'Pygmaea Argentea'**
A variegated dwarf bush that excels as a focal point in the garden. Grow it in open sunshine to maintain the pale-edged foliage.

Left: **Chamaecyparis lawsoniana 'Tamariscifolia'**
A slow-growing compact bush that eventually develops a rounded form. It looks best set among large rocks.

Below: **Chamaecyparis obtusa 'Nana Gracilis'**
Widely used for bonsai culture, this lovely Japanese cultivar will grace any rockery with its distinctive sprays of rich, dark green foliage. Slow-growing, it needs well-drained soil.

Chamaecyparis pisifera 'Boulevard'

- Light shade
- Moist garden soil with not too much lime
- Quick-growing medium bush

This cultivar was raised from Japanese parents in the 1930s, and has become very popular. It has a compact conical or pyramid shape, and the silvery steel-blue foliage is particularly strong in summer. It grows quickly, reaching 2m/6.5ft tall by 1m/39in wide in ten years, and can be trimmed to keep a good shape without losing its character. In 20 years it could reach 4.5m/15ft in height, with a spread of 3m/10ft. To keep the brightness of the silvery leaves, plant it in light shade. The bush has small cones about 6mm/0.2in across, each with ten pointed scales.

It is very easy to strike cuttings, in a half peat and half sand mix. Plant rooted cuttings in nursery beds for three years, and then place in their final positions. The soil should be moist, and this variety will tolerate some lime; added peat, leaf-mould and bonemeal will provide nutrients for a healthy start.

Take care
Keep the young plants moist.

Left: **Chamaecyparis pisifera 'Boulevard'**
Quick-growing but easily trimmed to size, this conifer is justifiably popular for its steely-blue foliage. It prefers light shade.

Chamaecyparis pisifera 'Filifera Aurea'
- Open position
- Moist but well-drained soil
- Slow-growing large shrub

This shrub has been in cultivation for almost 100 years and was developed from plants imported from Japan. It eventually makes a shrub about 4.5m/15ft tall, although in ten years it reaches only 1m/39in high with a spread of 1.2m/4ft. The foliage is distinctive, like threads of gold; the branches, trailing at their tips, give the whole plant a weeping look, which is particularly effective when the plant is on a rockery with some branches trailing down over lower levels. To keep the brightness of the foliage, plant the shrub in an open position. It bears 6mm/0.2in cones, which mature during the first year.

Propagation should be from cuttings, and it is recommended that, for a dwarfish plant with a trailing character, the cuttings should be taken from the weaker side shoots rather than the more vigorous leaders. After three years they can be planted in their final situations.

Take care
Keep seedlings weed-free.

Chamaecyparis pisifera 'Plumosa Aurea'
- Open situation
- Well-drained moist garden soil
- Fast-growing small tree

This small tree of Japanese origin is conical in shape, with densely packed branches. Its young foliage, bright yellow in colour, turns to yellow-green or bronze as it ages. The tree will grow to a height of 3m/10ft and have a spread of 2m/6.5ft in ten years, but it could eventually reach 8m/26ft. The leaves are coarser to touch than some plumosas, and if it has insufficient sun its gold may revert to green. The cones are 6mm/0.2in across, and ripen in the first year.

For a plant to be true to its parent, it should be grown from cuttings. These are taken in spring, and set in half peat, half sand. When they have rooted, move them to a nursery bed for three years, then plant them in their final positions. Choose an open site with a moist but well-drained soil that has some peat, leaf-mould and bonemeal added to give the plants a good start; they should establish themselves quickly.

Take care
Keep young plants moist.

Above: **Chamaecyparis pisifera 'Plumosa Aurea'**
This quick-growing small tree shines with colour in a sunny position. In ten years it will only grow to a height of 3m/10ft.

Left: **Chamaecyparis pisifera 'Filifera Aurea'**
Use this slow-growing shrub as a focus on a lawn. It needs direct sunlight in order to maintain its distinctive golden colouring.

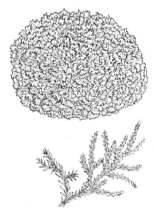

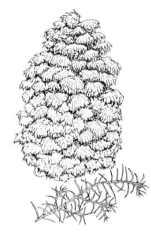

Chamaecyparis pisifera 'Snow'
● Sheltered position with light shade
● Ordinary moist soil
● Slow-growing dwarf bush

This small conifer was raised in Japan, and has pale green foliage with white tips, giving the appearance of a dusting of snow over the plant. It will make a compact bush that gradually develops a more open and fern-like look. The bush reaches a height of 2m/6.5ft if conditions are suitable; otherwise it may reach only half this size, and if given a rockery situation with a constricted root area it can be kept quite small. The cones are only 6mm/0.2in wide, and take up to a year to ripen.

Plants should be propagated from cuttings, set into a mixture of half peat, half sand in spring. When they are rooted, move them to a nursery bed for three years, and keep the bed weeded to prevent the young plants from becoming choked. The plants can then be transplanted to their final positions, which should be in light shade and sheltered from the wind.

Take care
Full sunlight and cold winds can burn the foliage so plant in a sheltered location.

Cryptomeria japonica 'Bandai-sugi'
● Open situation or light shade
● Moist, slightly acid soil
● Slow-growing compact bush

It is curious that this odd dwarf cultivar should have come from the large and majestic Japanese cedar. It will grow to about 1m/39in tall and wide in ten years. A mixture of tight moss-like foliage and normal leaf growth gives it an unusual appearance. The leader growth can be strong with slight side shoots, and this, together with the leaf structure, gives it a haphazard look that some gardeners find ideal for a focal point on a rockery. The cones are just over 1.2cm/0.5in wide, and remain on the tree for almost two years before turning brown and releasing their seeds.

Propagation should be by cuttings; side shoots should be taken, to keep the cuttings less vigorous. Set in half peat, half sand until rooted, then plant out into a nursery bed for two years.

Normally this bush is pest-free, but watch for grey mould on young plants; if seen, spray with a suitable fungicide such as zineb.

Take care
Keep young plants moist and free from weeds.

Cryptomeria japonica 'Elegans'
● Open or slightly shaded site
● Slightly acid, moist soil
● Small tree, grows fast at first

Brought out of Japan in 1854, this tall plant has a bushy appearance. The young soft foliage is kept throughout the plant's life, but turns from the summer blue-green to bronze or purple in winter. The tree grows quite quickly, and reaches 3m/10ft by 1.2m/4ft in ten years; then it slows down, to reach 12m/39ft in about 70 years, according to the soil. There is a compact form called 'Elegans Compacta' or 'Elegans Nana'. Cones develop on the tips of the shoots, and stay on for over a year to ripen from green to brown.

Sow seeds in spring in seed compost, and move the seedlings into a nursery bed when they are 7.5cm/3in tall. Select the best-coloured specimens only, and grow on for two or three years, then make a final selection for form and colour before planting out into position.

Normally this tree is pest-free, but watch for grey mould on seedlings, and spray with a fungicide.

Take care
Clear heavy snow off branches.

Right: **Cryptomeria japonica 'Bandai-sugi'**
*The combination of tight moss-like foliage and
normal leaf growth gives this dwarf, slow-growing
Japanese cultivar a unique appearance.*

Below: **Cryptomeria japonica 'Elegans'**
*This upright small tree changes in colour from
blue-green during the summer to bronze or
purple in the winter months. It grows quickly at
first and then slows down.*

Below: **Cryptomeria japonica 'Spiralis'**
Twisted ringlets of dense bright green foliage adorn this slow-growing bush. Originating in Japan, this variety can form either a bush or a tree. Prefers an open or lightly shaded position.

Right: **Cryptomeria japonica 'Vilmoriniana'**
The tight green foliage of this dwarf bush turns reddish-purple in the winter. In ten years it will reach only 40cm/16in in height and is ideal as a subject for the rock garden,

Far right: **Cunninghamia lanceolata**
This conifer forms a graceful tree with long pointed leaves. It is a suitable specimen for planting in the centre of a lawn, where it can grow steadily to a height of 4m/13ft in ten years.

Cryptomeria japonica 'Spiralis'
(Granny's ringlets)
- Open or lightly shaded site
- Slightly acid, moist soil
- Slow-growing bush

This plant was brought out of Japan in 1860. It normally forms a shrub about 50cm/20in in height and width in ten years, with dense bright green leaves twisted around the branches to give a ringlet look. Sometimes, however, the plant forms a large tree, and if this occurs it can drown the surrounding planting. The cones are borne on the tips of the branches and take over a year to ripen from green to brown.

If the seed is sown, keep only the dwarf slow-growing seedlings to grow on to maturity. The best method is to grow from cuttings, using the less vigorous side shoots and setting them in a half peat, half sand mixture. When they are rooted, plant in pots for a year and then set out in nursery beds for two years. Select the best forms and plant them out in the final positions, using a deep moist soil that is slightly acid.

Usually this bush is free from pests, but spray it with a fungicide to deter grey mould.

Take care
Keep young plants moist.

Cryptomeria japonica 'Vilmoriniana'
- Open or lightly shaded site
- Well-drained but moist soil
- Slow-growing dwarf bush

This popular dwarf bush for the rockery has little in common with its Japanese ancestors. It has very small crowded foliage on tiny branches that form into a globe. In ten years it will reach only 40cm/16in tall with a spread of 50cm/20in; in 30 years it should grow to 60cm/2ft tall and 1m/39in wide. The foliage is a rich green for most of the year, but turns reddish-purple in winter. Cones form at the ends of the branches, and ripen during the following year, turning from green to brown in colour.

Propagate this bush from cuttings to keep plants true to type. They should be set into a half peat, half sand mixture, and the rooted cuttings put into pots for a year, then set out into nursery beds for a further year or two before being transplanted into their final situations. An open site or one with light shade is suitable.

These plants are usually free from pest attacks, but spray seedlings with fungicide to deter grey mould.

Take care
Keep young plants moist.

Cunninghamia lanceolata
(China fir)
- Needs a sheltered position
- Ordinary well-drained soil
- Medium- to quick-growing tree

This tree comes from southern China, where it grows to a height of 25m/82ft, but in cultivation it should reach only about 4m/13ft high and 2m/6.5ft wide in ten years. The foliage grows down to ground level, giving the appearance of a coarse spruce; the leaves, however, are much bigger – up to 6cm/2.4in long – and of a glossy dark green. The shape makes this tree particularly suitable for a lawn specimen. The cones are carried on the branch tips and are about 5cm/2in in diameter, turning from green to brown as they ripen.

The seed can be sown in a seed compost in spring, and the seedlings transplanted to a nursery bed in autumn, where they should be left for three years before planting out in their final positions. Choose an open site sheltered from strong wind, with ordinary garden soil enriched with peat, leaf-mould and bonemeal.

Normally the China fir is both pest- and disease-free.

Take care
Avoid a windy site.

Left: **Fitzroya cupressoides**
This will form a fairly compact bush if it is kept pruned. One of its particular attractions is that the rusty-brown bark peels off to reveal the grey trunk underneath. Needs an open situation.

Fitzroya cupressoides

- **Open situation**
- **Any well-drained soil**
- **Medium to large shrub or slow-growing tree**

In its native Chile and Argentina this species will grow 50m/164ft tall and 9m/29.5ft wide, but in cooler areas the plant will be smaller and if pruned can be kept to a bush form. The foliage consists of scale-like leaves 6mm/0.2in long set in threes around the stems, and the extremities of the branches have a weeping effect. The cones are small, about 8mm/0.3in across, with nine scales; they change from green to brown as they ripen, and remain on the tree through the winter, splitting to release the seed. The dark rusty-brown bark peels off to show the grey trunk that lies underneath.

The seed can be sown in a seed compost, and the seedlings put out into a sheltered nursery bed for two or three years, then transplanted into their final positions. Choose an open site with a well-drained soil enriched with peat, leaf-mould and bonemeal. These plants are normally free from attacks by pests and diseases.

Take care
Protect seedlings from cold until they are fully established.

Juniperus chinensis 'Aurea'

(Golden Chinese juniper)
- **Open or light shade**
- **Most garden soils**
- **Slow-growing small tree**

This yellow-foliaged cultivar is very slow-growing to start with, but quickens later to form a slender column-like tree. It will grow to 1.5m/5ft tall and 80cm/32in wide in ten years, and matures to about 6m/20ft tall with a width of 1m/39in. The plant bears two types of foliage: the juvenile has needle-like leaves, and the adult ones are scale-like, which gives the plant a two-toned effect. The cones take the form of berries, and ripen in the second year, when the seeds can be extracted in autumn and sown.

To achieve a good colour and form it is better to take cuttings, setting them in a mix of half peat and half sand in a cold frame. Transplant rooted cuttings into a nursery bed for two years and then plant out into their permanent sites in ordinary soil. Some growers prefer to graft cuttings on to a healthy stock. Spray plants with malathion to prevent scale insects, and zineb to stop rust.

Take care
Avoid sites with too much sun.

Above: **Juniperus chinensis 'Aurea'**
This golden juniper comes from the Far East and is celebrated for the combination of juvenile needle-like and adult scale-like foliage, which gives the plant a two-tone effect.

Juniperus chinensis 'Kaizuka'

(Hollywood juniper)
- **Any situation**
- **Most soils**
- **Large shrub with a medium rate of growth**

This has become very popular due to its upright shape, its bright green foliage and its ability to grow virtually anywhere. The branches are long and spreading, following no set pattern, and it makes a good contrast next to neat and tidy plants. It will grow to 3m/10ft tall with a width of 1.2m/4ft in ten years in a warm site; in cooler areas it is less vigorous. The berry-like cones take over a year to ripen.

The seed can be sown but it is better to grow plants from cuttings. These should be taken in autumn, put into a mixture of half peat and half sand, and transplanted into a nursery bed when rooted. After two years move to their permanent positions. Choose an ordinary soil, even shallow chalk, and add peat, leaf-mould and bonemeal to give a good start. To prevent scale insects spray the plant with malathion, and to stop rust infection spray with zineb.

Take care
Keep pruning cuts hidden behind foliage to retain appearance.

Juniperus chinensis 'Obelisk'
● **Most situations**
● **Ordinary soil**
● **Slow-growing medium shrub**

This plant forms a narrow, slightly irregular column, with bluish-green foliage that often looks paler by the exposure of the whitish undersides of the leaves. These are densely packed and needle-like. This juniper reaches a height of 3m/10ft with a width of 80cm/32in when fully grown, but at ten years will have reached only 1m/39in tall. Cones are in the form of berries, which ripen in the second year.

The seed can be taken out and sown, but cuttings retain the colour and form of the parent more truly. Take cuttings in autumn, and set into a half peat and half sand mixture in a cold frame. When rooted they should be planted out into a nursery bed for two years, and then into their permanent site. Choose an ordinary soil with peat, leaf-mould and bonemeal added. The location is not critical, as they tolerate most sites. Spray with malathion and zineb to keep the plants free from pests and diseases.

Take care
Keep young plants free from weeds.

Right: **Juniperus chinensis 'Obelisk'**
A columnar conifer, slightly irregular in form, its foliage has a blue-green tinge, complemented by the white undersides of the leaves.

Juniperus chinensis 'Pyramidalis'

- Grows in most positions
- Ordinary garden soil
- Slow-growing medium bush

This slow-growing conifer forms a dense cone-shaped bush that reaches 2m/6.5ft in height and 1m/39in wide in ten years, but when fully grown will reach 5m/16.4ft tall and 2m/6.5ft wide. The needle-like foliage is prickly, and blue-green in colour. The rounded cones are 6mm/0.2in wide.

The seeds can be sown in a seed compost in autumn and placed in a cold frame; plant out seedlings into nursery beds when large enough to handle. From a batch of seedlings select the best colours and forms to grow on. After two years move the plants to permanent positions. Choose a well-drained garden soil in full sun or light shade, and add peat, leaf-mould and bonemeal to assist the young plants to establish themselves quickly. Otherwise grow from cuttings set into an equal mix of peat and sand, and grow on as seedlings when rooted. Spray with malathion and zineb to keep the plants free from pests and diseases.

Take care
Keep young plants moist.

Juniperus communis 'Compressa'

- Light shade or full sun
- Most soils, including chalk
- Dwarf slow-growing shrub

This cultivar of the common juniper looks like a miniature Irish yew tree, forming a tiny narrow column that reaches only 40cm/16in tall in ten years, with a width of 10cm/4in, and has a mature height of about 80cm/32in. It grows barely 5cm/2in a year, which makes it an ideal plant for rockeries and also for sink and scree gardens. The miniature needle-like foliage is dark green and very closely set on the upright stems. The cones are small and will ripen during the second year.

Propagate by taking cuttings, setting them in a half peat, half sand mixture until rooted. Transplant into pots of potting compost and grow on for two years before planting out in final positions. They tolerate most soils, including chalk, and are happy in full sun or light shade. Spray with malathion to stop attack by scale insects and red spider mite, and also with zineb to deter fungal attack.

Take care
Watch for red spider mites.

Above: **Juniperus chinensis 'Pyramidalis'**
A slow-growing medium-sized conifer which forms a dense cone-shaped bush. It is suitable for most positions in the garden. The needle-like foliage is blue-green.

Left: **Juniperus communis 'Compressa'**
A slow-growing dwarf conifer that forms a narrow column. It is ideal for rockeries, containers and scree gardens, where its neat shape and dark colour show to advantage.

Left: **Juniperus communis 'Depressa Aurea'**
This prostrate variety may eventually grow to a width of about 3m/10ft, its golden-leaved shoots spreading out just above soil level.

Juniperus communis 'Depressa Aurea'
● Full sun
● Most well-drained soils
● Slow-growing prostrate shrub

This is a dwarf wide-spreading bush; the branches grow just above the soil with the tips curving downwards. It reaches 1.2m/4ft wide and 30cm/1ft tall in ten years, and an ultimate width of over 3m/10ft. This plant has needle-like leaves; in the spring the young foliage is bright yellow, dulling to a bronze colour by the autumn. It makes a fine specimen plant for a rockery or for a sunny border. The cones are berry-like and very small, 6mm/0.2in wide, and these turn black as they ripen during their second or even third year on the tree.

This shrub is best propagated from cuttings, which will keep the colour and habit of the parent. Set them into an equal peat and sand mixture until they have rooted, and then move to nursery beds (allowing for them to spread horizontally); after two years plant them out to their final site. Spray with malathion and zineb to keep pest and disease attack to a minimum.

Take care
For good colour, keep in the sun.

Juniperus communis 'Hibernica'
(Irish juniper)
● Full sun or light shade
● Most garden soils
● Slow-growing large shrub

This excellent narrow column-like shrub will make a fine plant for a formal arrangement. Its very upright form needs no training or trimming to keep its shape; it grows to a height of 2m/6.5ft with a width of 40cm/16in after ten years, and the final height is almost 6m/20ft. This is too large for the average rockery, but it is a good plant for a border or a focal point in the garden. The needle-like leaves are closely positioned on the branches. The cones are berry-like, turning black as they ripen during the second or third year.

Grow from cuttings to keep the form true. These should be set into a half peat, half sand mix; when rooted, transplant into pots or a nursery bed to grow on for two years before moving to their final situations. Choose a well-drained soil in sun or light shade. Spray the plants with malathion and zineb to keep them free from pest and disease attack.

Take care
Shake off excess snow during the winter.

Juniperus communis 'Hornibrookii'
● Full sun or light shade
● Most garden soils
● Slow-growing dwarf spreading shrub

This plant forms a low creeping plant that follows the contours of the ground. It will spread to over 1.2m/4ft across with a height of 25cm/10in in the first ten years, but as it grows older it will slow down its spread and increase in height. The sharply pointed needles are grey-green with a silvery underside.

It can be grown from cuttings taken in the autumn; set them into a half peat and half sand mixture, and when rooted plant out into nursery beds with at least 20cm/8in between the cuttings to allow for spread. Leave them to grow for two years before planting out into their permanent positions. Choose a site that is open and sunny or in light shade, with ordinary well-drained soil; add some peat, leaf-mould and bonemeal to give the plants a good start. Spray with malathion and zineb to prevent attack by red spider mites, scale insects or diseases.

Take care
Keep the young plants weeded and moist until they are established.

Above: **Juniperus communis 'Hornibrookii'**
A slow-growing and wide-spreading shrub which is eminently suitable for rockeries and as a ground cover plant. Needs sun or light shade.

Left: **Juniperus communis 'Hibernica'**
A fine plant for formal settings, with a distinctive columnar shape and tight needle-like foliage. Plant in full sun or light shade.

75

Above: **Juniperus conferta**
This adaptable juniper will grow in most soils, including salty sand. It develops at a medium pace into a spreading prostrate shrub.

Left: **Juniperus horizontalis 'Wiltonii'**
A splendid dense blue conifer which can be grown to provide good ground cover. The colour turns a little deeper with colder temperatures.

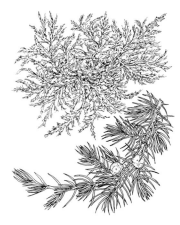

Juniperus conferta
- Full sun
- Most soils, particularly salty sands
- Medium-growing prostrate shrub

This sea-shore plant forms a low-growing shrub that over a period of ten years will spread to 2m/6.5ft wide and a height of about 30cm/1ft in the centre, while the outer stems will hug the ground. The leaves of this shrub are bright apple-green needles with a white band on the upper surface. The round cones are approximately 1.2cm/0.5in across, and these will turn black when they are ripe.

Although this shrub can be grown from seed, it is usual to propagate it by cuttings; take these in autumn and set them in an equal mix of peat and sand. When they are rooted, move them to a nursery bed to grow on for two years before planting them out in their final positions. They thrive in full sun and in most soils; a good deal of sharp sand is beneficial in heavy soils and the addition of peat, leaf-mould and bonemeal will help the plant to get established. Spray this shrub with malathion in order to prevent it being attacked by scale insects, and also with zineb to cut down disease.

Take care
Keep young plants moist.

Juniperus horizontalis 'Wiltonii'
(Wilton carpet juniper, Blue rug)
- Full sun or light shade
- Ordinary garden soil
- Slow-growing prostrate shrub

This cultivar forms a dwarf shrub with long branches that hug the ground, eventually forming a dense mat of foliage making it suitable for ground cover. It will grow to 1m/39in across in six years, and 1.5m/5ft in ten years, with a height of 15cm/6in. Its foliage is bright blue, and it is regarded as the best of the blue prostrate junipers; the colour turns a little deeper with winter temperatures.

This shrub is mostly grown from cuttings, taken in the autumn and set in a half-and-half mixture of peat and sand. When they have rooted, plant in pots or in a nursery bed for two years before planting them out in their final positions in the garden. These plants should be grown in an open sunny site or in light shade, in ordinary garden soil; you will find that added peat, leaf-mould and bonemeal will encourage good root growth. Spray with malathion and zineb to kill pests.

Take care
Keep young plants weed-free.

Juniperus x media 'Hetzii'
(Hetz blue juniper)
- Full sun or light shade
- Ordinary well-drained soil
- Medium to large shrub

This hybrid forms a medium to large shrub with rising branches and a silvery blue-green scale-like foliage that gives it a smooth touch. It will form a bush 2m/6.5ft tall and as wide in ten years, and eventually it will reach about 3m/10ft tall and the same wide.

It is best propagated from cuttings taken in autumn and set in a mixture of half peat and half sand; the rooted cuttings are then planted out into nursery beds, where they should stay for two years. Plant into final positions where there is full sun or light shade; the soil should be ordinary well-drained garden soil, and addition of peat, leaf-mould and bonemeal will encourage healthy root growth.

To lessen the chances of scale insect attack, spray the plants with malathion. Watch for caterpillars of the juniper webber moth and treat with the same spray. Use zineb to cut down diseases.

Take care
It is important to keep young plants moist during drought periods.

Right: **Juniperus** x **media 'Hetzii'**
This medium to large shrub has silver-blue foliage and a strong shape that recommend its use in large rockeries and borders, where it will be in scale with other plants.

Left: **Juniperus** x **media 'Old Gold'**
A wide-spreading shrub which, unlike some varieties, retains its superb golden colour throughout the year. Grow in full sun.

Right: **Juniperus** x **media 'Pfitzerana'**
An extremely popular cultivar prized for its irregular spreading habit. It needs a well-drained soil but tolerates sun or light shade.

Bottom right: **Juniperus procumbens 'Nana'**
This dwarf prostrate shrub looks very effective on rockeries. It is also useful for training over walls or unsightly objects.

Juniperus x media 'Old Gold'
- Full sun
- Ordinary well-drained soil
- Slow-growing medium shrub

This forms a shrub as high as it is wide, with ascending branches, giving it the look of a golden explosion. It will grow to 1.5m/5ft wide by 70cm/28in tall in ten years (although it can form plants of 1m/39in wide and high in the same period), with a final size of some 2.4m/8ft wide and 2m/6.5ft tall. The golden scale-like leaves stay bright during winter, instead of fading like some varieties.

Grow from cuttings taken in autumn and set in a half peat and half sand mix; the rooted cuttings are then grown on in a nursery bed for two years before being planted out in their permanent situations. Select the best for colour and form. Use an open site with plenty of sun to keep a bright gold colour; an ordinary well-drained soil fortified with peat, leaf-mould and bonemeal will suit the plants well. Spray with malathion and zineb against pests and diseases.

Take care
Keep plants in the sun for a bright gold colour.

Juniperus x media 'Pfitzerana'
(Pfitzer juniper)
- Full sun or light shade
- Well-drained garden soil
- Wide-spreading medium bush

This is probably one of the most popular conifers grown. It is an excellent plant for formal or informal gardens, with its wide-spreading habit that can reach 2m/6.5ft across by 1m/39in high in ten years. The branches rise at an angle with a drooping tip; the whole bush has an irregular shape, with scale-like leaves of a fresh green. It is often used for covering man-holes and septic tanks, and although on the large size for the average rockery, it can be used there as a centre point around which other plants are grouped.

Grow it from cuttings taken in autumn, and set into a half peat and half sand mixture. When rooted, the best specimens should be planted out into a nursery bed for two years and then moved into their final situations. Grow in a well-drained soil, in sun or shade; peat, leaf-mould and bonemeal are helpful to the young plants.

Take care
Keep seedlings weed-free.

Juniperus procumbens 'Nana'
(Dwarf Japanese juniper)
- Sunny position
- Well-drained garden soil
- Medium-growing dwarf shrub

This creeping plant will spread to 1.2m/4ft across, with a centre height of 30cm/1ft, to make a ground cover like a green carpet. It looks good in a rockery, is also grown for bonsai, and can be trained to cover walls or objects. The needle-like foliage is bright green in spring, but gradually changes to blue-green as it matures. In cultivation there are no cones.

Cuttings should be taken in autumn and set into an equal mix of peat and sand. Over-winter in a cold frame, and in the following spring the best rooted cuttings can be put out into a nursery bed for two years; keep the soil free from weeds. Place in their permanent positions on a sunny site with a well-drained soil, and keep the young plants weeded. The soil can be improved with peat, leaf-mould and bonemeal, which encourage good root growth.

Take care
Keep the young plants moist.

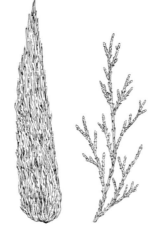

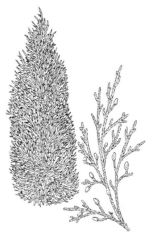

Juniperus sabina 'Tamariscifolia'
- Sun or light shade
- Most well-drained soils
- Wide-spreading shrub

This shrub has a distinctive form, with branches arching out of the centre, each branch with vertical stems spreading along its length. It will grow to 1.5m/5ft wide and 50cm/20in tall in ten years; if conditions are right it may eventually grow to several metres wide, but it can be kept smaller by pruning. The needle-like leaves are bright green. The rounded berry-like cones are 6mm/0.2in across.

The seeds can be sown in a seed compost; when they are large enough to handle, put them into a larger pot for a year, then move to a nursery bed for two years. Alternatively, plants can be grown from cuttings set in a mixture of half peat and half sand until rooted, and then moved to a nursery bed for two years. Plant out into a well-drained soil, in sun or light shade. To give protection against pests and diseases, spray these conifers with malathion and zineb.

Take care
Prune to the required size.

Juniperus scopulorum 'Skyrocket'
- Sunny position
- Well-drained garden soil
- Medium-to slow-growing small tree

This is probably the most narrow of the upright conifers in cultivation, being only 30cm/1ft wide and 2m/6.5ft tall after ten years, and 5m/16.4ft tall but still only 30cm/1ft wide after 20 years. It is very popular as a vertical plant for use as a contrast wherever there is a flat horizontal scheme, such as a heather garden or a large paved area. The scale-like foliage is silvery blue-green in colour.

To get the best plants, propagate from cuttings. These are taken in autumn and put into a half-and-half mixture of peat and sand. Over-winter in a cold frame, and then transplant the rooted cuttings into a nursery bed, keeping the soil well weeded. After two years move them into their final situations. Pick a sunny position with a well-drained soil, improved by digging in peat, leaf-mould and bonemeal to encourage good roots. Spray with malathion and zineb.

Take care
Keep young plants free of weeds.

Juniperus scopulorum 'Gray Gleam'
- Sunny position
- Well-drained soil
- Slow-growing small tree

This plant forms a narrow column that grows to about 1.2m/4ft tall and 30cm/1ft wide in ten years. The silvery grey-blue foliage seems to become more silvery in the winter months. The leaves are scale-like, and the red-brown trunk shreds into papery strings. It is excellent for a rockery or as an accent tree in a border or lawn, and its unusual colour makes it an all-the-year focal point in the garden. The plant is male and therefore does not bear cones.

Propagation under nursery conditions is by grafting on to a suitable stock. They are grown on as pot or container plants for several years, which accounts for their high price. Plant out into a sunny position, in a freely draining soil; the addition of peat, leaf-mould and bonemeal will encourage a good root structure. Spray with malathion and zineb to keep down pests and diseases.

Take care
Plant in well-drained soil.

Far left: Juniperus sabina 'Tamariscifolia'
A distinctive variety with arching branches, bright green needle-like leaves and rounded berry-like cones. If left undisturbed it will spread widely but it can be kept small by pruning.

Left: Juniperus scopulorum 'Skyrocket'
An extremely narrow conifer that provides a vertical contrast where there is a horizontal planting scheme such as a heather garden or on a large paved area.

Below: Juniperus scopulorum 'Gray Gleam'
This American cultivar develops slowly into a small tree with a columnar shape and silvery grey-blue foliage. It is excellent as an accent tree in a border or on a lawn.

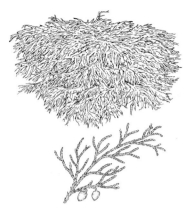

Juniperus squamata 'Blue Star'
● Sunny situation
● Well-drained soil
● Slow-growing dwarf bush

This new variety forms a small low shrub with quite large needle-like leaves packed on the short stems; the intense silvery-blue colour gives it great impact. After ten years' growth it makes a globe 40cm/16in in diameter; its ultimate size is still a matter for conjecture, but some experts estimate 1m/39in tall with a slightly greater spread. The berry-like cones are just over 6mm/0.2in wide.

Grow from cuttings taken in autumn and set into a half peat and half sand mixture. Overwinter in a cold frame, then set out in a nursery bed to grow on for two years. Plant out in final positions in a well-drained soil in full sun, keeping the young plants weeded and clear of overshadowing plants. Apply a mixture of peat, leafmould and bonemeal in order to encourage good, strong growth. To keep plants free from pest and disease attack, spray with malathion and zineb.

Take care
Keep young plants well weeded.

Juniperus squamata 'Meyeri'
(Meyer juniper)
● Full sun
● Well-drained garden soil
● Small to medium bush

This plant makes an irregular bush with arching and ascending branches that dip at the tips. It will form a bush about 2m/6.5ft high and wide in ten years, and may eventually reach 5m/16.4ft; it can be pruned to make a more compact plant. The needle-like leaves are steel-blue in colour; then they turn brown but stay on the tree for several years before falling. The cones are like berries, 6mm/0.2in wide.

The seeds can be sown in a seed compost but there is likely to be wide variation. It is better to grow from cuttings, taken in autumn and set into a half-and-half mix of peat and sand; keep in a cold frame over winter. Transplant the rooted cuttings into a nursery bed in spring, and grow on for two years. Plant out into permanent positions, choosing a well-drained soil enriched with peat, leaf-mould and bonemeal. In order to keep the blue colour, grow this plant in a sunny position in the garden.

Take care
Prune hard to keep plant small.

Juniperus virginiana 'Grey Owl'
● Sunny situation
● Most soils
● Medium-growing low to medium shrub

This plant has widely spreading branches of a yellow colour that contrasts well with the grey-green foliage. The plant will spread in ten years to 1.5m/5ft wide and 45cm/18in tall, with a dense centre but more open towards the extremities, with more pronounced thread-like stems and scale-like leaves. It is seen at its best against a dark background.

To keep a good colour and form it is best to grow new plants from cuttings. These are taken in autumn, set into a half peat and half sand mix and kept in a cold frame over winter. The rooted cuttings are then planted out into nursery beds for two years before moving to their final positions. Place them in an open sunny situation in well-drained soil enriched with peat, leaf-mould and bonemeal. Spray these plants with malathion and zineb in order to prevent attack by pests and diseases.

Take care
Hard pruning will ensure that the plant is kept small and dense.

Right: **Juniperus squamata 'Blue Star'**
Grown for its intense silver-blue colour and dwarf globe-like shape, this is a fairly new variety. It is slow-growing with needle-like leaves.

Above: **Juniperus virginiana 'Grey Owl'**
This wide-spreading shrub benefits from hard pruning to retain a good shape. The yellowish stems contrast well with the grey-green foliage.

Left: **Juniperus squamata 'Meyeri'**
Regular pruning will keep this fairly vigorous conifer in check and encourage an attractive bushy shape. It thrives in full sunshine.

Left: **Picea abies 'Clanbrassilliana'**
A slow-growing flat-topped bush, its green foliage becomes noticeable in winter due to the appearance of brown winter buds.

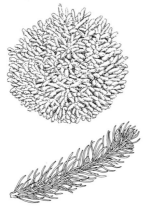

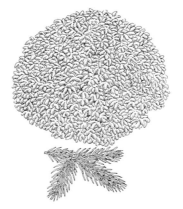

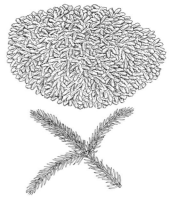

Picea abies 'Clanbrassilliana'
● **Sun or light shade, but not an exposed site**
● **Deep moist soil**
● **Slow-growing small bush**

This plant makes a low round flat-topped bush in the early stages, and matures as a dense round-topped shrub. Growth is slow; a ten-year-old plant reaches 80cm/32in in height and spread, and it grows to a height of 1.2m/4ft and a width of 2.4m/8ft after 40 years. The foliage is green and becomes very noticeable in winter because of the numerous brown winter buds. Cones are about 10cm/4in long and hang downwards; they fall in their second year.

Seeds can be sown in a seed compost, and the seedlings transplanted when 7.5cm/3in tall into a nursery bed, where they should stay for two or three years. At this stage, select only the best plants, and move them to permanent positions. Choose an open or lightly shaded site that is not exposed to cold winds, with a deep moist soil, preferably slightly acid. This bush is ideal for rockeries and borders.

Take care
Keep young plants moist.

Picea abies 'Little Gem'
● **Sun or light shade**
● **Deep moist soil**
● **Slow-growing dwarf bush**

This plant makes a round bun-shaped dwarf bush that is very slow-growing, reaching only about 30cm/1ft tall and wide in ten years, with a possible ultimate size of 60cm/2ft tall and a spread of 1m/39in. The leaves are small and densely packed on to the shrub. It is ideal for a rockery, or a sink or scree garden.

Seeds can be sown, but careful selection must be made to keep the form and colour of the parent. Cuttings are best taken under nursery conditions; they need to be kept in protected nursery beds for at least two years before being planted out into their final positions. Grow in an open sunny or lightly shaded site that is not exposed to cold winds. The soil should be moist and slightly acid; feed with phosphate and nitrogen in spring and summer. Spray plants with malathion and zineb to deter pests and diseases.

Take care
Protect young plants against cold winds.

Picea abies 'Nidiformis'
● **Sun or light shade**
● **Deep moist soil**
● **Slow-growing dwarf spreading bush**

This cultivar makes a flat-topped dense dwarf bush with an inclination to grow outwards rather than upwards. In ten years it spreads 70cm/28in with a height of 25cm/10in; in 20 years it has a width of 1m/39in, and is 30cm/1ft tall. The branches rise at first as they spread, but then droop at the tips. The leaves are green, and the young growth in spring is apple-green. This plant makes a good shrub for a rockery or border, or it can be grown in a container. The cones are green and ripen to brown in autumn.

The seeds can be sown in pots, then moved to nursery rows and grown on for two years. Before planting out into their final positions, choose the best for size and colour. Plant in a deep moist soil that is slightly acid, in sun or light shade. In spring feed with a phosphate and nitrogen fertilizer. To keep plants free from pests and diseases, spray with malathion and zineb.

Take care
Cold winds damage young plants.

Right: **Picea abies 'Little Gem'**
This dwarf cultivar develops into an appealing compact mound of bright green foliage. Young plants should be protected from cold winds.

Below: **Picea abies 'Nidiformis'**
This slow-growing dwarf cultivar is suitable for a rockery, a container or a small border. For best results plant in sun or light shade.

Picea abies 'Reflexa'
(Weeping Norway spruce)
- Sun or light shade
- Deep moist soil
- Wide-spreading slow-growing shrub

This variety normally makes a low-growing shrub with long prostrate branches, but can be trained to form a weeping tree that makes an excellent specimen for a lawn. The rate of growth is slow – about 12.5cm/5in a year – and a 25-year-old shrub will spread to 4m/13ft across, with a height of 50cm/20in in the centre. The leaves are neatly formed into furry-looking tails of mid-green. This somewhat curious plant really needs a slope or large rock ledge on which to grow. The cones are about 10cm/4in long.

The seeds can be sown in pots and then transplanted to nursery beds, where they are grown for two years. Select for colour and form, and move the most weeping specimens to their permanent positions. Plant in deep moist soil, preferably slightly acid, and in sun or light shade. To keep pests and diseases at bay spray plants with malathion and zineb.

Take care
Cold winds damage young plants so afford them some protection in their early years.

Picea glauca albertiana 'Conica'
(Dwarf Alberta spruce)
- Full sun or light shade
- Moist deep soil
- Slow-growing dwarf bush

This plant makes a perfect cone shape of soft dense grass-green foliage. It will make a bush with a height of 80cm/32in and a width of 30cm/1ft at the base in ten years; it reaches 1.2m/4ft tall and 75cm/30in wide in 20 years, with an ultimate height of about 3m/10ft. However, the plant can be trimmed to fit the available space. The cones are brown when ripe and are about 2.5cm/1in long.

The seeds should be sown in pots in spring, and put out the following year into nursery beds for two years. Choose the best forms and colours to plant out into their final positions. Select an open site in full sun or light shade, with a deep moist soil on the acid side. The young tree has a peak growth rate in spring and summer, when a feed of phosphate and nitrogen is beneficial. Spray with malathion and zineb to deter attacks by pests and diseases.

Take care
Water young plants in droughts.

Picea mariana
(Black spruce)
- Open sun or light shade
- Deep moist soil
- Medium tree of medium growth

This medium-sized tree normally makes a height of 9m/29.5ft in cultivation, but often reaches 30m/98ft in the wild. As a cultivated plant it may be short-lived unless conditions are right, and it keeps a conical shape instead of the tall columnar form of its natural state. In ten years it should grow to 2.4m/8ft high with a width of 1.5m/5ft; in 20 years it makes a tree 4.5m/15ft tall with a spread of 3m/10ft. The stems are densely packed on the upper surfaces with dark blue-green needles, which when crushed emit an aroma of menthol. Cones are borne in large numbers; they are 3.7cm/1.5in long, and dark purple, turning brown.

The dwarf form 'Nana' makes a very slow-growing bun shape, 30cm/1ft tall with a spread of 60cm/2ft, ideal for the rockery.

Seeds can be sown in pots and grown on for three years before planting out into a deep moist soil, in sun or light shade.

Take care
Keep young plants moist.

Bottom far left: **Picea abies 'Reflexa'**
A wide-spreading and slow-growing shrub with a drooping habit. It can be trained to form a weeping tree which looks striking set on a lawn.

Bottom left: **Picea mariana 'Nana'**
This is a very slow-growing dwarf cultivar which forms a bun shape. It is perfect for rockeries as it only reaches 30cm/1ft in height.

Below: **Picea glauca albertiana 'Conica'**
This magnificent plant develops slowly into a fine cone shape of densely packed foliage. It will grow to an eventual height of 3m/10ft.

Left: **Picea orientalis 'Aurea'**
This forms a medium-sized conical tree or bush with pale yellow foliage which turns to gold in the summer. It needs a shady location.

Picea orientalis 'Aurea'
- Shady site
- Deep moist soil
- Medium-sized tree, slow-growing at first

This golden-foliaged form of the Oriental spruce is slow-growing at first, but after about 15 years it increases its rate of growth unless it is planted on shallow or dry soils, where it will be short-lived. It forms a medium-sized conical tree or bush, which reaches 3m/10ft in height and 1.2m/4ft wide at the base in ten years, but in 20 years can reach 9m/29.5ft in height and 4.5m/15ft across, and ultimately 13.5m/44ft tall in ideal conditions. The foliage is pale yellow when young, turning in summer to gold, and eventually to green. A dwarf cultivar, 'Aurea Compacta', tends to burn in hot sun but makes a fine plant for a shady location.

The seeds can be sown in spring in pots, and planted out when large enough to handle. Keep only the bright golden seedlings to grow on in nursery rows for two years. Select the best specimens and plant out into a deep moist soil, in full sun.

Take care
Select plants for colour and form.

Picea pungens 'Globosa'
- Open sun or light shade
- Deep moist soil
- Small slow-growing bush

This cultivar of the Colorado spruce has a dwarf habit and forms an irregular shape, often flat-topped. It makes a bush 50cm/20in tall and 70cm/28in wide, with blue-grey needles. It is excellent for rockeries, sink gardens or borders. In spring the young growth appears in pale blue tufts on the ends of the branches and contrasts with the darker blue of the older leaves. The pale cones are cylindrical in shape with pointed scales, about 10cm/4in long, and these eventually ripen to a shiny brown.

The seeds can be sown in pots in spring; transplant the seedlings to nursery beds for two years, and keep the beds well weeded. Select the best specimens: bluer foliage and smaller plants are preferable. Plant out into deep moist soil in sun or light shade. Feed young plants with phosphate and nitrogen in spring and summer. Spray with malathion and zineb to keep down pests and diseases.

Take care
Water young plants in dry weather.

Picea pungens 'Koster'
(Koster's blue spruce)
- Open sun
- Deep moist soil
- Small to medium tree

This is the most popular of the blue spruces, because of its intensely blue foliage, its neat habit of growth and its ability to fit into formal and informal gardens. It grows with an upright pyramidal shape to 2m/6.5ft tall and 1m/39in wide in ten years, with an eventual height of some 9m/29.5ft with a spread of 3m/10ft in good conditions. Tassels of blue leaves are enriched with pale blue tufts when new growth breaks in spring. Cones are about 10cm/4in long, with pointed scales, and ripen to a pale brown colour.

Propagation is preferably by grafting good leader material on to a *P. pungens* stock to encourage a good upright form; this makes the plant scarce and expensive. Growing from seeds gives a wide variation in both colour and form. Plant in a good deep moist soil in open sun. Spray with malathion and zineb to prevent pest and disease attack.

Take care
Keep young plants moist.

Above: **Picea pungens 'Globosa'**
A cultivar of the Colorado spruce, this has a dwarf habit and forms an irregular shape. It is excellent for sink gardens or borders.

Right: **Picea pungens 'Koster'**
This is one of the most popular of the blue spruces because of its intense colour, neat pyramidal form and the spectacular pale blue tufts of fresh spring growth. It will fit well into many garden situations.

Right: **Picea pungens 'Pendula'**
With careful training and pruning this unpredictable cultivar can be persuaded to develop a fine weeping shape. It can provide an excellent focal point in a sunny site.

Picea pungens 'Pendula'
- Open sun
- Deep moist soil
- Slow-growing small tree

This cultivar, which is sometimes referred to as 'Glauca Pendula', is erratic and needs careful training to give it a distinct shape. It tries to produce both leaders growing vertically and horizontal weeping branches, which makes the plant look confused, but pruning and training will make it an exciting and attractive focal point in any garden. It is difficult to give a true size for such an unpredictable plant, but it could reach up to 5.5m/18ft in height and spread. The blue foliage has paler tufts of new growth on the tips in the spring. The cones are 10cm/4in long, with pointed scales, and these will ripen to a pale brown colour.

Propagation is by grafting to keep the true character of the parent plant; this is done by taking a cutting from the parent and grafting it on to a *P. pungens* stock. Plant in the open in a deep moist soil. In order to keep the plant in the best of health, it is advisable to spray with both malathion and zineb.

Take care
Train to make a good shape.

Picea pungens 'Thomsen'
- Open sun
- Moist deep soil
- Small to medium tree

This cultivar has a good upright habit of growth. The branches are packed with silvery-blue needles that are thicker than other forms. It makes a conical tree some 2m/6.5ft in height and 1m/39in wide at the base in ten years, with an ultimate height of 9m/29.5ft and a width of 3m/10ft given the right growing conditions. The spring growth forms tassels of palest silver-blue that contrasts with the older and darker foliage. Cones are 10cm/4in long, with pointed scales, and these will eventually ripen to a shiny brown. The bark is grey, and as it ages it breaks up into rough plates.

Propagation is by grafting leader shoots on to a *P. pungens* stock; this ensures that the upright form and fine colour of the parent plant are maintained. Plant in the open, in a deep moist soil; a feed of phosphate and nitrogen in spring and summer is beneficial. Spray plants with malathion and zineb to keep them pest- and disease-free.

Take care
Keep young plants moist.

Pinus aristata
(Bristlecone pine)
- Open sun
- Good deep garden soil
- Small tree or large shrub of slow growth

This tree is slightly irregular in form, with upright branches densely packed with blue-green needles. It will eventually make a tree about 10m/33ft tall but certainly not in the lifetime of the planter; it can therefore be treated as a rockery or border subject, with an average growth rate of 5cm/2in a year. The needles are in bunches of five with pale inner surfaces. The cones are 7.5cm/3in long, and each scale has a distinctive long bristle attached.

Seeds should be sown in pots in spring, and kept in a cold frame; plant out the seedlings the following spring into a nursery bed. Grow on for three years keeping the bed well weeded, and then plant out into final positions. Choose an open site with good soil, preferably slightly acid. Keep moist initially, but these plants are drought-resistant when established. Spray with malathion and zineb in order to cut down on pest and disease attack.

Take care
Keep young plants moist.

Above: **Pinus aristata**
A very slow-growing pine that has the distinction of being the oldest living tree species in the world. Plant it in a deep soil as a dwarf rockery plant and expect only 5cm/2in of growth a year.

Left: **Picea pungens 'Thomsen'**
This is another fine blue spruce which is suitable for the average garden. The foliage is thick and the needles long. It will grow steadily into a strong upright shape.

91

Pinus densiflora 'Umbraculifera'
(Umbrella pine)
- ● Open situation
- ● Ordinary soil
- ● Slow-growing dwarf tree

This dwarf cultivar of the Japanese red pine makes an umbrella-shaped or flat-topped tree, with branches radiating out from the trunk like umbrella ribs. The plant is very slow-growing; it reaches less than 1m/39in in height and spread in ten years, and in 30 years it makes a tree only twice this size. These trees are prized as mature plants in containers, and command high prices for instant landscape projects. The dense foliage is a rich green, with long needles in pairs, about 7.5cm/3in long and twisted. The small cones are produced while the plant is still young.

Seeds can be sown in pots of seed compost, kept for a year in a cold frame and then planted out into a nursery bed. After two years, transplant the seedlings into their permanent positions. Grow in ordinary soil in full sun. Treat with malathion and zineb to deter attacks by pests and diseases.

Take care
Keep young plants watered.

Pinus heldreichii leucodermis 'Compact Gem'
- ● Open position
- ● Dry shallow chalk soil
- ● Slow-growing dwarf bush

This cultivar is a very slow-growing pine with upright tufts of needles in an irregular form. It will make a bush about 1.2m/4ft tall by 1m/39in wide in 20 years. It may have an ultimate height of 1.8m/6ft and a spread of 1.2m/4ft, depending on soil and climatic conditions. The dark green needles are in pairs, and are densely packed on the stems. Cones are dark purple, ripening to golden brown in their second year, and about 5cm/2in long.

It is advisable to obtain grafted specimens, as seed growing results in wide variation. Grafts are taken in spring, a section of the parent plant being grafted on to a suitable stock. In this way the plant is true to its parent in form and colour. Plant in an open space, in a dry shallow chalk soil. It is a good idea to add some moisture-retentive material such as peat or well-rotted compost to give the plant a good start. An annual feed of a general fertilizer is beneficial.

Take care
Keep young plants well weeded.

Pinus mugo 'Gnom'
- ● Sunny site
- ● Most soils, even lime
- ● Slow-growing dwarf shrub

This very popular dwarf shrub is much in demand for rockeries, scree gardens and containers where it can be admired to best advantage. The plant makes a dark green bun shape, 80cm/32in wide and 50cm/20in tall, in ten years. It has a densely bushy structure, and the paired needles, 3.7cm/1.5in long, are set closely on the branches. In the spring the fresh growth gives the appearance of whitish candles; these pale needles will gradually turn green and blend in with the previous growth. The small cones are 2.5cm/1in long.

If the seed is sown it is unlikely to grow true. The plant is normally increased by grafting a section of the parent plant on to a rootstock of *Pinus mugo*, and in this way the dwarf character is sustained. Plant out in the late autumn or (if mild) during the winter. Grow in ordinary soil – it will tolerate chalk – and place in full sun. To keep the plants healthy, spray them with both malathion and zineb.

Take care
Keep young plants watered.

Far left: **Pinus densiflora 'Umbraculifera'**
Highly prized as a container plant, this slow-growing dwarf pine produces radiating branches in the shape of an umbrella. It will bear cones as a young plant. It needs an open situation.

Left: **Pinus heldreichii leucodermis 'Compact Gem'**
A slow-growing pine which prefers a dry and shallow chalky soil. It develops into a dwarf bush of irregular conical shape with dark foliage.

Below: **Pinus mugo 'Gnom'**
Useful for rock gardens and containers, this dense bush produces pale young shoots in spring which resemble candles. It needs a sunny site but tolerates most soils.

Pinus mugo pumilio

(Dwarf Swiss mountain pine)
- Full sun
- Most soils, even chalk
- Slow-growing dwarf bush

This plant is widely used in rockeries and scree gardens, where its miniature bun shape of light yellow-green makes a focal point. It grows very slowly, making a mound 40cm/16in across and 25cm/10in tall in five years; in ten years it could reach 50cm/20in across and 30cm/1ft high. The needles are closely packed in pairs on the short stems; in spring, when the fresh growth appears, the tufts of pale yellow-green give the plant a speckled look. The small cones are 2.5cm/1in long, and turn brown when ripe.

The seeds can be sown in pots. Keep in a cold frame for a year, and then make the first selection of plants for slow growth and good colour. Grow on in a nursery bed for two years, and then make a further selection to keep only the best. These are planted out in the open in ordinary soil, and will tolerate a chalky soil. Spray with malathion and zineb.

Take care
Keep young plants weed-free.

Pinus nigra 'Hornibrookiana'
- Open position
- Ordinary soil
- Very slow-growing dwarf bush

This plant is a dwarf cultivar of the Austrian pine, with a spreading ground-hugging character. A ten-year-old bush would be about 90cm/3ft wide and 35cm/14in tall. The foliage is a dark rich green, prickly to the touch and grouped in pairs. It looks its best in spring when the young growth forms – first light brown buds, and then the needles emerge with a pale fresh green. The cones are small.

The seeds should not be sown, or the resulting plants will revert back in character to the large Austrian pine. It is advisable to graft a shoot from the parent plant on to a rootstock of *Pinus nigra* to keep the dwarf habit. Plant in an open position; it will grow in most soils, including chalky ones. It withstands wind and salty air, so it is eminently suitable for seaside locations. The plants are occasionally attacked by pests and diseases, and it is therefore wise to spray with malathion and zineb as a precaution.

Take care
Water young plants in droughts.

Pinus parviflora

(Japanese white pine)
- Open sun
- Garden soil
- Slow-growing small to medium tree

This is the pine tree in the famous 'Willow Tree Pattern'. It forms a slow-growing bushy tree with a flat top when mature, when it should be about 10m/33ft tall; in ten years it will reach only 1.5m/5ft in height with a similar spread. It can be used in bonsai. The foliage is blue-green with blue-white inner surfaces. The needles are curved, giving the plant a very lively appearance; they are grouped in fives, and are spread sparsely along the stem. The 5cm/2in cones ripen from green to brown and will remain on the tree for several years.

The seeds can be sown in a seed compost in pots in spring; grow on in a cold frame for a year and then plant out into a nursery bed. After two years lift the plants and move them to an open site with ordinary garden soil. Spray the plants with malathion and zineb to deter pest and disease attack.

Take care
Keep the young plants weeded.

Left: **Pinus mugo pumilio**
In spring this charming dwarf conifer has a speckled appearance as fresh shoots of palest yellow-green contrast with the darker mature foliage. Highly recommended for rock gardens and containers. It will tolerate full sun.

Above: **Pinus parviflora 'Adcock's Dwarf'**
*Congested clusters of grey-green needles are
borne at the shoot tips of this dwarf conifer. It
develops slowly into a compact small tree.*

Left: **Pinus nigra 'Hornibrookiana'**
*This sturdy variety will thrive in almost any
situation, including windy seaside sites, and on
almost any soil, including chalk. It grows slowly.*

Pinus pumila 'Globe'
- Sunny site
- Ordinary garden soil, not chalky
- Slow-growing dwarf bush

This cultivar from *P. pumila* forms a slow-growing dwarf plant with a bushy habit. In 20 years one can expect a plant about 60cm/2ft tall and equally wide, of densely packed brushes of blue-grey needles. The needles, which grow up to 10cm/4in long, are grouped in fives and the plant looks most effective when the young growth starts in spring. The cones appear while the bush is still quite young; they are oval and grow to 5cm/2in in length.

The seed is unlikely to grow true, reverting instead to the *P. pumila* character of growth. Plants are produced in the trade by grafting cuttings taken from the parent plant on to a rootstock such as *Pinus strobus*; in this way the true form, colour and character of growth will be ensured. Place in a good light soil (but without lime) in full sun. Once established, this bush will be drought-resistant. Spray with malathion and zineb.

Take care
Keep young plants from being choked by weeds.

Left: **Pinus pumila 'Globe'**
The bushy form of this dwarf conifer makes it perfect for rockeries, scree gardens and containers. Avoid chalky soils for best results.

Pinus strobus 'Nana'

(Dwarf white pine)
- **Open position**
- **Ordinary soil**
- **Slow-growing dwarf shrub**

This shrub has a very slow rate of growth and a dense compact shape, which makes it ideal for rockeries, sink or scree gardens and borders. The plant is likely to grow to 50cm/20in tall and equally wide in ten years, and will reach about 1m/39in high and across in 20 years. The needles are in groups of five, blue-green and up to 20cm/8in long. The plant is usually grown by taking a cutting of 'Nana' and grafting it on to a seeded rootstock of *P. strobus*; grown on for several years it makes a good plant, and this accounts for the high price one has to pay. There are some variations in the plants sold as 'Nana', some being more dwarf and slower growing than others. Choose a good plant with a closely packed habit, as this will be a better specimen; they are not widely stocked but are worth searching for. Plant in the open in ordinary soil. Spray with malathion and zineb.

Take care
Keep young plants well weeded.

Pinus sylvestris 'Aurea'
- **Sunny position**
- **Ordinary soil**
- **Slow-growing small tree**

This small slow-growing tree is noticeable for its golden winter foliage. It forms a conical tree with a slightly irregular profile, growing to 2m/6.5ft tall with a spread of 1m/39in in ten years, and may eventually reach 6m/20ft. It is a good tree for the small garden, where it should not outgrow the space available. The foliage is quite densely packed when young; the new needles are blue-green in spring, taking on a yellow cast in summer, and becoming golden in the winter. The needles are in pairs and are approximately 5cm/2in in length.

The tree should be propagated by grafting, to keep the golden quality of the foliage and the slow growth. Plant the young pines out into ordinary soil; they will not do well if the soil is dry and chalky, or damp and acid. Spray with malathion and zineb to prevent pest and disease attack.

Take care
Keep young plants watered in periods of dry weather.

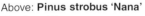

Above: **Pinus strobus 'Nana'**
The long blue-green needles of this slow-growing dwarf shrub clothe the sturdy branches in attractive dense clusters. It is widely planted in rockeries and borders.

Left: **Pinus sylvestris 'Aurea'**
This attractive cultivar develops slowly into a small tree. The new needles, blue-green in spring, become tinged with yellow in summer and turn gold during the winter months.

97

Left: **Pinus sylvestris 'Beuvronensis'**
A superb miniature cultivar for borders and rockeries. The new growth forms 'candles' of fresh green above the grey-green needles of the mature foliage. It needs an open situation.

Pinus sylvestris 'Beuvronensis'
● Open situation
● Ordinary soil
● Slow-growing small shrub

This miniature Scots pine was developed from a malformation on a normal tree (called Witches' Brooms). By using one as a cutting it is possible to obtain a plant with a different growth habit. This form makes a compact dome-shaped shrub that in ten years will grow to only 60cm/2ft tall, with a spread of 1m/39in. In its early stages it is quite small and needs protection from overhanging plants. It should grow eventually to over 2m/6.5ft tall with a width of 3m/10ft. The paired grey-green needles are about 2.5cm/1in long, and the shrub is densely branched. The new growth in spring looks like candles.

The stock is increased by grafting, and the new plants are kept in pots for at least four years before being planted out into ordinary soil in an open situation. Sometimes the plants are kept in pots until they are large enough to face competition from other plants.

Take care
Keep young plants in pots for several years before planting out.

Pinus sylvestris 'Fastigiata'
● Open situation
● Ordinary garden soil
● Slow-growing small tree

This cultivar of the Scots pine has a most unusual shape for this family, as it is very narrow for its height. Slower growing than the Scots pine, it should make a height of 2.5m/8ft with a width of 60cm/2ft in ten years; on maturity it reaches about 10m/33ft tall but less than 1m/39in wide. It is one of the hardiest narrow conifers available. The foliage is blue-green; the needles grow in pairs and are about 5cm/2in long, on closely packed upright branches. The spring growth of new leaves has the effect of candles on the branch ends.

This plant is in very short supply, due to problems of propagation, although it has been grown since the 1850s. Cuttings need to be grafted on to a rootstock and kept under nursery conditions for at least four years to ensure that the graft is good. Plant out in an ordinary soil, in full sun. The plants should be sprayed with malathion and zineb in order to deter pests and diseases.

Take care
Keep young plants well weeded.

Above: **Pinus sylvestris 'Fastigiata'**
This cultivar grows slowly into a tall narrow shape. It tolerates cold weather better than other narrow conifers and will thrive in ordinary garden soils. The foliage is blue-green.

Left: **Pinus sylvestris 'Viridis Compacta'**
This rather curious dwarf plant has long twisted needles that give it an unkempt appearance. It matures slowly into a rounded, medium-sized shrub. Grow it in full sunshine.

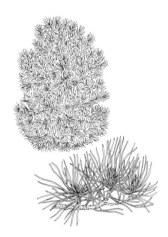

Pinus sylvestris 'Viridis Compacta'

- ● **Full sun**
- ● **Ordinary soil**
- ● **Slow-growing medium shrub**

This dwarf form of the Scots pine is more of a curiosity than a fine pine specimen. When young it has the appearance of a shaggy green hedgehog, but as it grows it takes on a more complex form. It reaches a rough rounded shape about 1.5m/5ft tall with a spread of 75cm/30in when mature, but in ten years could be expected to make 75cm/30in in height with a width of 50cm/20in. The foliage is bright grass-green in colour, and the 10cm/4in twisted needles are tightly packed in pairs.

This plant is normally propagated by grafting on to a rootstock, and it is kept under nursery conditions to make sure that the union is satisfactory before being sold. The plants should be grown in an open site with ordinary garden soil. Where the soil is in doubt, add plenty of peat or compost to improve it. Spray the plants with malathion and zineb to cut down the attacks by pests and diseases.

Take care
In dry soils, keep the young plants moist until established.

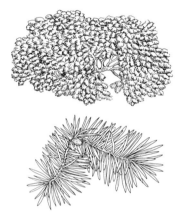

Pinus sylvestris 'Watereri'
● Sunny position
● Ordinary soil
● Slow-growing small tree

This slow-growing Scots pine has blue foliage and a rounded form. It will take many years to reach maturity; a 100-year-old specimen has reached 7.5m/25ft tall and as wide, but for the ordinary garden it should be regarded as a dwarf plant, and should grow to 1.5m/5ft tall with a similar spread in ten years. It has an upright growing habit that, with the blue foliage, makes it a striking plant for a rockery or border. The needles are in pairs around the stems, and in spring the tree is enhanced by the candles of young growth.

This plant should be increased by grafting cuttings on to a rootstock. Keep in a pot for several years under nursery conditions, and select only the healthiest plants. These should be planted on an open sunny site with ordinary garden soil. The addition of peat and compost will improve the plant's growth. Spray with malathion and zineb.

Take care
Keep young plants well weeded.

Pseudotsuga macrocarpa
(Large-coned Douglas fir)
● Open situation
● Moist well-drained soil
● Medium tree of medium growth

This tree will reach 25m/82ft where conditions are good, but can be dwarfed to 9m/29.5ft if the roots are constricted and there is a lack of nutrition. The tree should make 4.5m/15ft in growth in the first ten years, with a spread of just over 2m/6.5ft. The needle-like foliage is 2.5cm/1in long, narrow, green and slightly curved. The cones are up to 18cm/7in long and hang downwards. The bark is grey with wide brown vertical fissures.

The seed should be sown in pots in spring, kept in a cold frame and, when the seedlings are large enough to handle, moved to a nursery bed for two years. Transplant out into their permanent positions where there is a deep moist but well-drained soil that is not chalky. An area of high rainfall is excellent. Keep the ground around the young plants free from weeds. Spray with malathion and zineb to deter pests and diseases.

Take care
Keep young plants well weeded.

Pseudotsuga menziesii 'Fletcheri'
● Open position
● Deep moist well-drained soil
● Slow-growing dwarf shrub

This plant is also called *P. glauca 'Fletcheri'*. It forms an irregular round bush with a flat top and may eventually reach 2m/6.5ft high and wide. In ten years a plant 35cm/14in tall and with a similar spread can be expected; it will reach 60cm/2ft in both height and width in 20 years. This size makes it ideal for a rockery or border, where it can grow undisturbed for years. The dense foliage is arranged on each side of the branch, with short blue-green needles; in spring the plant has a spotted effect as the pale buds open on the branch ends. It can be pruned to shape.

This tree rarely produces cones; propagate by either cuttings or grafting. The young plant should be kept under nursery conditions for several years to ensure that the graft is satisfactory or the cutting healthy. Plant in an open position with a moist well-drained soil, preferably acid or neutral.

Take care
Keep young plants watered.

Right: **Pseudotsuga macrocarpa**
In fertile, moist and well-drained soil this species will grow steadily if the roots are not constricted. In small spaces root pruning will be needed.

Below: **Pseudotsuga menziesii 'Fletcheri'**
A popular slow-growing dwarf shrub which grows to a height of 2m/6.5ft over 20 years. This size makes it ideal for the rockery or border.

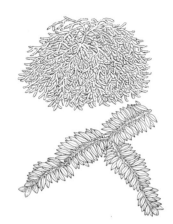

Sequoia sempervirens 'Prostrata'

● Open position or light shade
● Ordinary moist soil
● Slow-growing dwarf shrub

This is a cultivar of the world's tallest tree, but in size bears no resemblance to it. It tends to grow sideways rather than upwards, to form a slow-growing dwarf bush thickly covered in blue-green leaves. The plant should reach 10cm/4in tall with a spread of about 60cm/2ft in ten years, if encouraged to grow as a prostrate plant; but it can be trained to form a bush with more height than spread. The eventual size is unknown, as it has been in cultivation for only 30 years. The foliage is densely packed on the stems in two ranks of scale-like leaves.

The plants are grown from cuttings taken in autumn; set them in a half peat, half sand mixture, and place in a cold frame until spring. Move rooted cuttings to a nursery bed for two years, then plant out into their permanent positions. They will grow in shade but perform better in the open. Normally they are trouble-free.

Take care
Young plants are prone to frost damage on the stem tips.

Right: **Sequoia sempervirens 'Prostrata'**
A spreading cultivar tending to grow sideways rather than upwards, it can be trained to form a bush if desired. Tolerates sun or light shade.

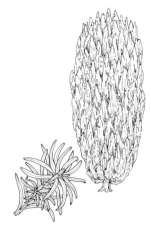

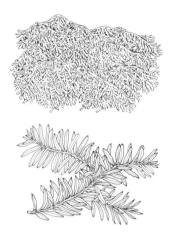

Taxus baccata 'Fastigiata Aurea'
(Golden Irish yew)
- Open site
- Well-drained soil
- Slow-growing large shrub

This shrub has a very neat upright form, and golden leaves. It forms a narrow bowl shape with very tight foliage, which gives it a solid look. A ten-year-old plant will reach to a height of 2m/6.5ft tall with a spread of 76cm/26in, and it will eventually reach 4.9m/16ft high. The foliage is a glorious yellow-gold, holding its colour right through the winter.

Propagate by cuttings in autumn; set them in a half-and-half mixture of peat and sand, and in the following spring move the rooted cuttings to a nursery bed. Grow on for two years and then plant out into their final positions. Choose a soil that is well-drained, either acid or alkaline, and in full sun to encourage a good gold colour. If using them for a hedge, plant at least 35cm/14in apart; a feed of a general fertilizer will give them a good start. Spray with malathion to deter pests.

Take care
This plant is poisonous.

Taxus baccata 'Repandens'
- Sun or shade
- Well-drained soil
- Low, slow-growing shrub

This makes a low wide-spreading bush, excellent as a ground cover plant. It is slow-growing, reaching 40cm/16in tall and 1.5m/5ft wide in ten years, and with an ultimate height of 1m/39in and a spread of 4m/13ft. The foliage is dense and tidy, with dark green leaves packed along the stems; the branches spread with a characteristic droop at the tips. This is a female shrub, and the berry-like cones turn bright red.

The seeds can be sown, but seedlings are unlikely to grow true. Take cuttings in autumn, set in a half peat and half sand mix, keep in a cold frame over winter, and plant out the rooted cuttings into a nursery bed in spring. After two years plant out into their final situations. Most well-drained soils are suitable, and the plant thrives in full sun or shade. Plant this shrub where children and animals cannot eat the leaves or berries as it is poisonous. Spray with malathion to keep pest-free.

Take care
This plant is poisonous.

Above: **Taxus baccata 'Fastigiata Aurea'**
A finely shaped golden shrub that retains its glorious yellow-golden colour all the year. It forms a narrow shape with very tight foliage.

Left: **Taxus baccata 'Repandens'**
A slow-growing prostrate cultivar that provides good ground cover. The branches spread with a characteristic drooping at the tips.

Left: **Taxus baccata 'Repens Aurea'**
Plant this low spreading cultivar in full sun to retain its brightness. The foliage is dense and each leaf is green with a margin of gold.

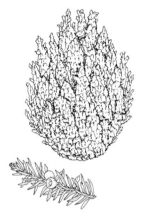

Taxus baccata 'Repens Aurea'

- Full sun
- Well-drained soil
- Slow-growing ground cover

This is similar in habit to *Taxus baccata* 'Repandens', but it also has variegated leaves. It grows slowly, to make a plant 35cm/14in high with a width of 1m/39in in ten years; over the years it reaches about 3m/10ft wide and 90cm/3ft tall. The spreading branches can be trimmed back to a domed shape. The foliage is dense, and each leaf is green with a margin of gold – pale gold in spring but gradually becoming deeper. The branches spread, with drooping tips.

Grow from cuttings taken in autumn, struck in a half peat and half sand mixture and over-wintered in a cold frame. In spring set the rooted cuttings in a nursery bed for two years. The plants should be placed in well-drained soil in full sun; shade would make the plant lose its golden colour and revert to green. This plant is poisonous so only grow it in an area without children or animals. To protect the plant from pest attack, spray it with malathion.

Take care
This plant is poisonous.

Taxus baccata 'Semperaurea'

(Evergold English yew)

- Full sun
- Well-drained soil
- Slow-growing medium-shrub

This golden-foliaged shrub makes a bush that is rather irregular in shape with upright branches densely packed with foliage. It grows 1m/39in in height and width in ten years, and ultimately reaches 3m/10ft tall and equally wide. The foliage is golden when freshly opened in spring, gradually becoming more browny-yellow through the year. The shape of the plant can be controlled by pruning or clipping.

The plant has no cones, as it is a male form, and has to be propagated by cuttings. These should be taken in autumn, set in a half-and-half mix of peat and sand, and over-wintered in a cold frame. In spring transplant the rooted cuttings into nursery beds for two years. Then move them to permanent positions in a well-drained soil, and in full sun to keep the gold colour of the foliage. Spray with malathion in order to keep the plants free from pests.

Take care
This plant is poisonous.

Taxus baccata 'Standishii'

- Open sun
- Well-drained soil
- Slow-growing medium shrub

This is a narrow upright form with golden foliage, and very slow growing. It makes an ideal subject for a rockery, container or scree garden. It is a cultivar of the Irish yew, with the same neat character and tight foliage. In ten years it could reach 70cm/28in tall with a spread of 15cm/6in, and its final size is just over 1.5m/5ft. The foliage is a beautiful gold, especially in winter, and closely hugs the upright branches, which lie tight to the central stem; the leaves radiate from the stem. Cones are borne as berries that ripen to a bright red.

To keep the character, this plant has to be propagated by cuttings, which should be taken in autumn, struck in a half peat and half sand mixture and grown in a cold frame over winter. Set out the rooted cuttings into a nursery bed in spring, and after two years move them to their final positions in well-drained soil in full sun to keep the colour.

Take care
This plant is poisonous.

Above: **Taxus baccata 'Semperaurea'**
*This golden cultivar will develop slowly into a
medium-sized bush. The yellow colour is most
intense on the new spring growth.*

Left: **Taxus baccata 'Standishii'**
*A narrow upright form with golden foliage, this
slow-growing conifer is a cultivar of the Irish yew,
with the same tight foliage.*

Above: **Thuja occidentalis 'Danica'**
This bun-shaped compact cultivar is perfect for a sunny rockery or equivalent site in a small garden. It grows slowly, its vertical sprays of bright green foliage forming a very neat and attractive shape.

Left: **Thuja occidentalis 'Holmstrup'**
This magnificent cultivar develops into a pyramidal bush up to 3m/10ft tall. The dense foliage retains a good green colour all the year.

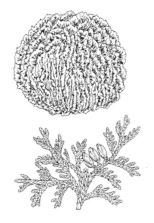

Thuja occidentalis 'Danica'
- Full sun
- Deep moist soil
- Slow-growing dwarf bush

This cultivar forms a small slow-growing bun that looks fine on a rockery or among heathers. It will grow to 30cm/1ft tall with a spread of 45cm/18in in ten years, and eventually reaches about 75cm/30in high and 1.2m/4ft wide. The scale-like foliage is carried on fans in vertical sprays, which gives it a very neat shape. The bright green leaf colour turns to bronze during the winter months, and if they are crushed the leaves will give off an apple-like scent. The cones are yellow-green, ripening to brown in the autumn, and are about 1.25cm/0.5in across.

To obtain plants with the characteristics of the parent, take cuttings in the autumn, set in a mixture of half peat and half sand, and keep in a cold frame during the winter months. Put rooted cuttings into pots of potting compost and plunge out of doors into a nursery bed for two years. Plant out in a sheltered position in full sun in a deep moist soil.

Take care
Keep young plants moist.

Thuja occidentalis 'Holmstrup'
- Full sun in sheltered position
- Deep moist soil
- Slow-growing medium bush

This cultivar forms a pyramidal bush that grows well in a border or rockery. At ten years old the plant will be about 1.5m/5ft tall with a width of 60cm/2ft across the base, and its ultimate height is around 3m/10ft. This slow-growing shrub has bright yellow-green foliage in closely packed fans of scale-like leaves. The leaves bronze slightly in the winter in cold areas, but this cultivar is one of the best to keep a green colour. The cones are green, ripening to brown, and 2.5cm/1in across.

The plants can be grown from cuttings taken in autumn, set into a half-and-half mixture of peat and sand, and kept in a cold frame over winter. Then put the rooted cuttings into pots and plunge these into a nursery bed for a period of two years. After this time transplant them into deep moist soil in a sheltered position in full sunshine. A spring feed of a general fertilizer and a mulch of peat and compost will help to keep the plants growing well.

Take care
Keep young plants weed-free.

Thuja occidentalis 'Rheingold'
- Full sun
- Deep moist soil
- Slow-growing large shrub

Regarded by some experts as one of the best golden leaved conifers, 'Rheingold' will make a low-growing shrub, with a flattened cone shape wider than it is tall, and of a fine gold colour. In ten years it will reach about 70cm/28in tall with a spread of 1.2m/4ft, with an eventual size of almost 4m/13ft across. This plant fits in well with heathers or on a large rockery. The foliage is densely formed of loose fans of golden scale-like leaves that smell fruity when crushed. During the winter, the gold darkens to copper. The plant can be trimmed to shape. Cones are 2.5cm/1in wide, and ripen from green to brown.

The plant is propagated from cuttings taken in autumn and put into a half peat, half sand mixture, kept in a cold frame until spring, and then potted. The pots are plunged into a nursery bed for two years. Then plant out into their final positions, in full sun and a deep moist soil. Usually these plants are trouble-free.

Take care
Keep young plants watered.

Left: **Thuja occidentalis 'Rheingold'**
A splendid golden-leaved conifer that grows slowly into a large shrub. During the winter the foliage takes on an appealing copper hue.

Far left: **Thuja orientalis 'Aurea Nana'**
A decorative slow-growing cultivar that retains its compact shape. It is a dwarf conifer which is suitable for rockeries or borders.

Left: **Thuja orientalis 'Elegantissima'**
Golden in summer, this cultivar turns bronze or green during the winter. It forms a conical column of about 1.5m/5ft in height.

Right: **Thuja plicata 'Rogersii'**
This dwarf golden conifer will suit rock gardens, heather gardens and containers. It thrives in a sunny position with deep and moist soil.

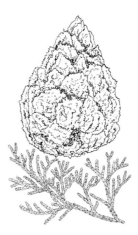

Thuja orientalis 'Aurea Nana'
- Full sun
- Deep moist soil
- Slow-growing small shrub

'Aurea Nana' makes a rounded cone shape of yellow-green that fits in with rockeries, borders, scree or heather gardens. It is a dwarf conifer growing to 60cm/2ft tall with a spread of 50cm/20in in ten years, and it rarely reaches higher than 1m/39in. The foliage is in vertical fans of densely packed scale-like leaves of yellow-green, which turn gold in winter. It will hardly ever need trimming. The small cones are approximately 1.8cm/0.7in wide, ripening from green to brown in the autumn, and have six hooked scales.

This plant is increased by cuttings. Take these in autumn, set into a half-and-half mixture of peat and sand, and over-winter in a cold frame. The rooted seedlings should be potted and sunk into a nursery bed for two years. Put out the plants into their final positions, ideally choosing a deep moist soil in full sun. Generally this shrub is trouble-free.

Take care
Plant in full sun for good colour.

Thuja orientalis 'Elegantissima'
- Full sun
- Deep moist soil
- Medium-sized shrub

This cultivar has golden tips to its green foliage; a good specimen looks like a golden conifer in summer, but turns green or bronze in winter. It forms a conical column about 1.5m/5ft tall, with a spread of 75cm/30in, in ten years, and will mature into a shrub 4m/13ft tall, with a spread of 1.8m/6ft. The sprays of scale-like leaves are held vertically. The colour is brighter if it is grown in full sunshine; in cold areas the foliage will brown in winter, but with protection it should keep a green colour. The cones are 1.8cm/0.7in wide and formed of six hooked scales.

Grow these plants from cuttings taken in autumn; set into a half peat, half sand mixture to root, and keep in a cold frame until spring. The rooted cuttings should be moved into a nursery bed to grow on for two years, and then transplanted to their final positions. Grow in a deep moist soil in full sunshine.

Take care
Choose a sheltered position.

Thuja plicata 'Rogersii'
- Sunny position
- Deep moist soil
- Slow-growing dwarf shrub

This dwarf plant has a fine conical shape and golden foliage, and is ideal for rockeries, scree or heather gardens or containers. In ten years this slow-growing plant will reach 70cm/28in high with a spread of 40cm/16in, and in 30 years it can grow over 1m/39in tall and almost as wide, but careful pruning will make a columnar form or wide-spreading bun shape. The fine foliage is densely packed in tight clusters, green in colour, with the edges of the scale-like leaf fans gold, and in winter this turns to bronze. Keep it in full sunlight to retain the gold.

Propagation is by cuttings, taken in the autumn. Set in a half-and-half mixture of sand and peat, and over-winter in a cold frame. In spring pot the rooted cuttings and plunge them into a nursery bed for two years. They can then be planted out into permanent positions in full sun and a deep moist soil. These plants are generally trouble-free.

Take care
Water young plants in droughts.

Below: **Thuja plicata 'Stoneham Gold'**
A compact golden cultivar which is extremely popular for its superb yellow-tipped sprays of foliage. In a sunny spot the colour lasts all year.

Thuja plicata 'Stoneham Gold'
- Full sunlight
- Deep moist soil
- Slow-growing small shrub

This plant's rich golden-yellow foliage is as bright in the winter as it is in the summer. In ten years this compact plant will have reached just over 70cm/28in tall and 35cm/14in wide; its ultimate size is estimated to be just over 2m/6.5ft. The foliage is dark green in the depths of the closely packed scale-like leaf sprays, but on the outer edges the colour pales to a bright orange-yellow. The plant can be trained to form a definite cone or ball shape.

The plant is grown from cuttings taken in the autumn and set in a mixture of peat and sand. It is important to keep these in a cold frame during the winter and pot up the rooted cuttings in the spring. Place them in a nursery bed for a period of two years and then plant them out in their final positions, which should be in full sunshine in a deep moist soil. These plants are usually free from pest and disease attack.

Take care
During dry weather, keep the young plants well watered until they have established strong root systems.

Tsuga canadensis 'Bennett'
- Partial shade
- Moist well-drained soil
- Slow-growing dwarf shrub

This plant is dwarf in character, making a low spreading plant with small yew-like leaves. It will grow slowly to just over 30cm/1ft tall with a spread of 60cm/2ft in ten years, and eventually makes a shrub about 1.2m/4ft high and 2.4m/8ft wide. The foliage is a fresh mid-green. The flat leaves are about 1.25cm/0.5in long, set in rows on either side and on top of the stem; these are crowded together to form a tight bush, with the branch tips slightly drooping.

The plant is propagated by cuttings in the autumn; set them in a half-and-half mixture of peat and sand and over-winter in a cold frame. In the spring place the rooted cuttings into pots and plunge them into a nursery bed for a period of three years. It is important to keep the bed clear of weeds, and also to water the young plants thoroughly during dry weather. Plant them out into a moist well-drained soil in partial shade, sheltered from dry winds. Normally this shrub is trouble-free.

Take care
Keep these plants moist.

Left: **Tsuga canadensis 'Bennett'**
This dwarf low-growing cultivar with its small yew-like leaves will thrive in moist well-drained soil. It will tolerate partial shade.

Tsuga canadensis 'Jeddeloh'

● **Partial shade**
● **Moist well-drained soil**
● **Slow-growing dwarf shrub**

This new cultivar makes a fine rockery plant, as it has a good lime-green colour and a semi-prostrate weeping habit, forming a flat bun-shape with a shallow hollow in the centre. As it is new, experts can only estimate its likely size; some say 50cm/20in tall and 1m/39in wide in ten years, but others say half this size, with an ultimate size of 1m/39in high and 2m/6.5ft across. The small flat leaves are ranged in rows along the sides and tops of the branches; these are densely packed, springing up and out from the centre, then curling down to give a neat shape of bright pale green.

The plant is propagated from cuttings; take these in the autumn, set into a half peat and half sand mixture, and place in a cold frame over the winter. In the spring pot the rooted cuttings and plunge them into a nursery bed for three years. Plant them out in shady positions in deep moist well-drained soil. These plants are generally trouble-free.

Take care
Weed and water young plants.

Tsuga canadensis 'Pendula'

(Weeping hemlock)
● **Sunshine or partial shade**
● **Moist well-drained soil**
● **Slow-growing medium shrub**

This plant has a distinctive habit of growth, forming a mound of overlapping weeping branches, and it makes a fine specimen plant for the lawn, or set high on a rockery. It forms a shrub 1.5m/5ft across in ten years; the height depends on whether the plant has been staked and trained, and with correct cultivation it should be around 1.5m/5ft tall, but if left untrained it will remain a prostrate shrub 60cm/2ft high. A good plant should grow to 3m/10ft tall and 9m/29.5ft across. The foliage is mid-green and looks magnificent with the spring growth of pale lime-green tips.

It is propagated by cuttings taken in autumn, set in an equal mix of peat and sand, and put into a cold frame until spring. The rooted cuttings are put into pots and sunk into a nursery bed for three years. Plant out into the open or in partial shade in moist well-drained soil. Generally this shrub is trouble-free.

Take care
Protect from drying winds.

111

Index of Common Names